GETTING YOUR AFFAIRS IN ORDER

GETTING YOUR AFFAIRS IN ORDER

How to arrange things to simplify your life
so that others can easily pick up where you left off

BY

EDWARD MENDLOWITZ, CPA/PFS/ABV/CFF

PARTNER, WITHUMSMITH+BROWN

iUniverse, Inc.
Bloomington

Getting Your Affairs in Order
How to arrange things to simplify your life
so that others can easily pick up where you left off

iUniverse books may be ordered through booksellers or by contacting:

iUniverse
1663 Liberty Drive
Bloomington, IN 47403
www.iuniverse.com
1-800-Authors (1-800-288-4677)

ISBN: 978-1-4620-7089-3 (sc)
ISBN: 978-1-4620-7090-9 (ebk)

Library of Congress Control Number: 2011961808

Printed in the United States of America

iUniverse rev. date: 12/15/2011

CONTENTS

EDWARD MENDLOWITZ, CPA

Edward Mendlowitz—CPA/ABV/CFF/PFS
Partner, WithumSmith+Brown

Ed is a partner in WithumSmith+Brown and is a member of the AICPA, NYSSCPA and NJSCPA and is accredited by the AICPA in business valuation, is certified in financial forensics and as a personal financial specialist. Ed is also admitted to practice before the United States Tax Court and has testified two times before the House Ways and Means Committee on tax reform and equity.

Ed serves on the NYSSCPA Estate Planning Committee, and was chairman of the committee that planned the NYSSCPA's 100th Anniversary. The author of 18 books, Ed has also written hundreds of articles for business and professional journals and newsletters. He is the contributing editor to the *Practitioners Publishing Company's 1998/1999 706/709 Deskbook*, the *AICPA* 2004 and current editions of the *Management of an Accounting Practice Handbook,* various editions including the first (1982) and most recent edition of the *Corporate Controllers' Handbook*, and the current edition of the *Handbook of Budgeting,* is on the editorial board of *Bottom Line/Personal* newsletter and is an editorial adviser on business valuation and litigation support for the *Journal of Accountancy*. He is the recipient of the Lawler Award for the best article published during 2001 in the *Journal of Accountancy*. Ed also has taught courses for 11 years in the MBA program at Fairleigh Dickinson University, and has spoken before business and professional groups for over thirty years.

Ed can be reached at emendlowitz@withum.com or 732 964-9329. His personal website is www.edwardmendlowitz.com.

ACKNOWLEDGEMENTS

No book is written solely by the author. It is the result of a long term collaboration with clients, partners, staff, colleagues, friends and acquaintances that probe, ask questions, need answers, have insecurities and constantly ask "what if."

It is impossible to acknowledge every contributor, simply because I am unable to call up from the recesses of my brain everyone that gave me an idea or thread that has been woven into the fabric of this book.

However, there are many that clearly come to mind and they include my partners Peter A. Weitsen, Frank R. Boutillette, William Hagaman, Jr., John Mortenson, Ron Bleich, Ruben Cardona, Howard Stein, Hal Terr, Ted Nappi and Don Scheier.

Others include Rich Maurer, Rick Famely, Kevin Fellin, Mary Jane Younghans, Joe Picone, Joan Paci, Debra Schmelzer, Walter Bialo, Richard Hochhauser and Joel Wilson.

Some of the material on insurance was provided by Thomas J Sharkey Jr, President of Meeker Sharkey Associates, LLC, Cranford, NJ.

My son, Andy Mendlowitz, a professional journalist and author edited the manuscript and presented many ways to have ideas flushed out and some difficult concepts simplified.

Everything I do, including this book, is done with the needed support and love of my wife Ronnie.

THIS IS A GUIDE—SEEK LEGAL ADVICE

Circular 230 wording

To ensure compliance with U.S. Treasury rules, unless expressly stated otherwise, any U.S. tax advice contained in this communication (including attachments) is not intended or written to be used, and cannot be used, by the recipient for the purpose of avoiding penalties that may be imposed under the Internal Revenue Code.

Caveat

This book is not intended to give legal or tax advice. It's purpose is to provide information. Anything you think might apply to you should be discussed with the appropriate professional. The reader is cautioned to seek legal counsel on any of the documents they need.

INTRODUCTION

Everyone's affairs end up the same way—distributed, dispersed or dumped.

Sometimes it is easy and sometimes difficult. The easier it is, the better the chance that the deceased's affairs are settled the way they wanted and with as little extra time and cost as possible.

This process starts with you, and can start today—or not at all. That is up to you.

This book will show you how to arrange your affairs so that you will have a better handle on your finances; your heirs will know what you want done and how; and possibly with as little distress to them as can be considering that this process is always upsetting because it injects memories of a loved one that is gone.

Arranging affairs is difficult because life interferes with a lot of "wish I could do's" or "need to do's." This book will lay out things you can do in an easy way to follow. The consequences of not following certain rules and, where applicable, laws are illustrated. For example, everyone has a will. It is either a will you cause to be written or the default will the state imposes on your estate. Neglecting doing something does not eliminate the need but rather says you prefer the way the state will dispose of your assets and that you won't mind the added costs, bother and time because you won't be around anyway.

Included here are worksheets and forms that can be filled in quite easily by you. If doing anything that needs to be done should prove difficult, think about the problems your heirs will have trying to find and assemble everything you had, or owed, and then report it to the governments involved and disburse the rightful shares to those you designated in the manner and at the time you determined.

Sometimes we look back and realize we would have liked to have done or said something better or different. Now is a good time to write it out as a final memo to those that were either affected or would have benefited. It can't change what was done, but might make the person appreciative of your thoughts. There is a chapter inside explaining what to do with final remarks.

CHAPTER 1

DECLUTTERING YOUR LIFE

Clutter robs you of time.

Think about how much time you waste looking for something. You pass over the same things time after time; you spend time to make room for more "good things" that you just have to have; or you spend energy looking at piles of stuff that you know "you'll need some day" but you never seem to have time for that "day" so the piles grow and grow and grow.

The one thing we have that is the same as everyone else is time, yet some seem to get so much more done, have so much more fun, and always seem ready to do something or go somewhere, while others just never seem to. The quantity of clutter is the difference between the doers and the never-get-to-doers.

I know many people, including myself, that never let go of anything. But I've also seen many friends move to what might be their final residences and somehow they get rid of tons of stuff. They are not any different than the accumulators—they just reached a stage in their lives where an uncluttered existence seems more preferable. I heard them all complain about having to get rid of their "valuable" accumulations, yet haven't heard any regrets afterward. There might just be something to uncluttering your live.

Clutter comes in many forms. Stuff becomes clutter. Unorganized stuff becomes even more clutter. Unmade "going to get to it" arrangements also inject clutter into your minds. This includes not making preparations for your death, hospital stays and prolonged rehab, potential incapacity, winding down your financial affairs, protecting yourself against bad unforeseen circumstances, and making sure what you want to occur with your assets, occurs the way you want it to.

Decluttering your life is not rocket science. But it takes resolve and movement. Wanting to do it doesn't work without the doing actually being done.

I have seen and heard about many houses of deceased loved ones being emptied of 50+ years accumulations of *Playbills*, *Reader's Digests*, *National Geographics* and *Harvard Business Reviews*. These treasures are tied and dragged to the curb to await the next recycling truck's visit. Someone will be throwing them out—it could be you or your family. As long as you have them, you have clutter, unless you regularly refer to a saved copy. And many libraries now have many of these available digitally, so anything you want to refer to is retrievable.

Making sound arrangements with a will, trusts, and other documents provides comfort and erase negative energy and possible anxiety and the quandaries presented by having to do something you just can't seem to want to do, get to, confront or decide. I can guarantee that if you can't make a decision about some things you should do, that decision will definitely be made someday, by someone and it won't be as good as your worst decision in the matter.

Decluttering also involves assembling all your important papers in one place, and consolidating bank and brokerage accounts. If you don't want to close any accounts, using Quicken® or Money® to aggregate your investing activities places all your information in one place making it easier to manage and for others, if necessary, to get a top side picture of your financial accounts. Another way to simplify your life is to sell small amounts of shares you have that, taken together, don't amount to much value. A bonus to this is that it will decrease the mail you get, most of which gets thrown out anyway. At a minimum, you will get mail at least five times a year for each stock you own. Selling ten stocks of less than a dozen shares owned in each of those companies will reduce your mail by 50 items a year—probably more since they also mail you repetitive offers to repurchase those odd amounts. Use the extra money to take your grandkids to the circus, or even buy them a car if you have enough from the sale. If you don't want to bother to sell them, donate the shares to your favorite charities and at least get a tax deduction out of it.

Speaking of charities, they regularly bombard us with address labels, calendars, note pads and even phone calls to get us to match others or do more. I hate to say you should stop contributing to them, but that seems to be the only way to get the harassment to stop—but it takes years. If you want to give, give through a blanket charity such as

United Way or through a major religious organization, or give cash to people you know that are raising money for worthwhile charities, and don't request a receipt, and don't provide your name and address. You will lose the tax deduction, which is a small price to pay to get rid of the scores of solicitations you get each month.

Other mail causing clutter are "contests" where you may have won a million bucks—you just have to send $22.95 to register your information. Once that is done—the mail and phone calls will start in earnest. You think the charity mail is harassment—wait until these people get you on their list.

Tax returns and the back up documents are excellent road maps of the accounts and investments you have. You should retain at least six years of tax returns and back up data. This way, someone handling your affairs or settling your estate would have a very good idea of what assets you have and where they are. One method to follow is to put each year's return and data in an envelope marked with the year on it, and the date you should dispose of it [shredding it, of course]. Each year when you put the information in the new envelope, get rid of the earliest one. Later in here is a listing of the types of records you should keep and for how long. You should review that also.

An important thing to do, if you still hold on to your stamp, coin, Lladro, whiskey shot glass, sugar package or match book collection is to leave instructions of who to go to that you believe is reputable and will make a reasonable offer for the accumulation, because that is what it is. If it were anything more, you would have won awards and then sold the collection at auction since you've already reached the pinnacle for that hobby. Organize whatever you retain so it will be easy to handle and identify the better and more valuable items.

Benjamin Franklin, a favorite of mine, said "do not squander time because that is the stuff life is made of." Clutter causes the squander. Declutter provides relief and an extra part of your life. Actually, Franklin began the quote with "Does thou love life?" You decide about the clutter!

CHAPTER 2

PURPOSES OF ESTATE PLANNING

Estate planning, also referred to as family wealth transfer planning, is a process that calls for a person arranging their affairs in an orderly concerted manner.

Estate planning is usually associated with saving estate and inheritance taxes, but that is not the primary reason. Estate planning is a method that provides for the testator (the person making the will) making their wishes clear and that transfers are made the way they wanted them made, and to whom, and when. I feel one of the most important reasons to plan and have a will is for parents to provide for a guardian for minor children should they die prematurely. And for that guardian to have adequate funds with which to carry out their unanticipated responsibility (this will be explained later)—this is not a tax savings issue, but a family security and growth issue.

Estate planning includes the following:

- To devise a plan that will provide for the financial security and comfort of the testator and their spouse for the balance of both their lives. This is not solely a plan for the remaining family after a death. Some might call this financial planning but it transcends the immediate issues and is involved with not outliving your money, hence leaving an estate.

- To have the testator and their spouse retain as much control and enjoyment as possible over their assets until their death.

- Keep the family assets in the family and out of the hands of creditors of family members and divorced spouses of family members if it applies.

- Figuring out what the estate taxes and administration costs will be and trying to minimize them and determine how they will be paid.

- Estimating the time probate takes; and to try to minimize unnecessary expenses and delays of probate and administration of the assets.

- Projecting the cash flow to the beneficiaries during the estate administration period and after the estate is settled.

- Helping the testator make the proper choices of bequests to their various beneficiaries including charities, if so desired.

- Helping the testator arrange their affairs so that it would be clear what state they are a resident of, if there is a chance that more than one state might make a claim.

- Arranging a plan of contingency for the operation and sale of any businesses.

- Setting up a methodology of liquidating non-liquid assets.

- Determining the applicability of trusts and arranging for their creation and funding.

- Determining the scope, if any, of liabilities the estate will have including notes signed and guaranteed, previous divorce settlements, prenuptial agreements, support commitments for children born out of wedlock, business buy sell arrangements and outstanding tax audits and liabilities.

- Determining the effect of income tax on some of the distributions and bequests, if applicable.

- Designate specific items of property to pass to certain people, such as a ring to a brother or niece.

- The will can be used to remember some people by leaving them fixed sums of money.

- Part of the process—and this has nothing to do with probate or taxes—is where the testator prepares a letter of instructions giving pertinent information they feel their family will need, or that will be helpful in the settling of their affairs. This letter tells what items need to be addressed immediately such as burial instructions and funeral information, people to notify, and the location of important papers.

- These letters also occasionally contain a statement of values or concerns that they want their children, grandchildren, or other heirs to know. The letter should be left in a place that would be looked at as soon as practical after death.

- Planning for the care of a disabled relative is super important if you are supporting someone in that position.

- The process helps put order into a person's affairs, collects and assembles information, and identifies and can clear up loose ends should they exist.

Chapter 3

Why a Will is Needed

Without a will, a state statute will designate who inherits the deceased's property and how it is distributed.

The estate of a person that dies with no will ("intestate") will have added costs because a court will need to appoint someone to oversee the administration of the estate. Related and interested parties will need to petition this appointee when they want, or need, something done or distributions from the assets. Additional costs will accumulate such as fidelity bond premiums, public notice ads and court appointed overseers' fees. Further, every extra action will add time and cause delays until the estate can make distributions.

And, very likely, the statutory distribution scheme (known as intestate distribution) will differ from the deceased's wishes.

Typically, intestate laws divide an estate between the surviving spouse and children, giving about one-third to one-half to the spouse and balance to the children, and possibly other relatives. Even if the decedent does not have children, the spouse generally will not inherit the entire estate.

Some people have everything in joint name, or a trust, or have all their assets, so they think, in accounts that have designated beneficiaries or inheritors. However, there is always something not included, or possibly someone that wants to make a claim against an estate causing the probate or surrogate court to initiate a file. If no assets come up, then this becomes a wasted exercise, but in some situations assets crop up. Some of these could be:

- a safe deposit box in decedent's name containing jewelry, gold coins or cash;
- personal jewelry, a watch or a family heirloom previously inherited by the decedent;
- cash on their person when they died in a public place;
- undeposited checks;
- unclaimed assets being held by the state through escheat laws;
- final pay checks, bonuses or commissions;
- a lottery ticket they purchased also on them when they died;
- money they lent someone;
- a stamp or coin collection;
- art and other valuable items; and
- various other assets that crop up unexpectedly.

For these people a simple will leaving everything to their spouse, or children will ease some inconvenience when they die. Another asset that can crop up is an inheritance by someone that predeceased them which they were unaware of, or where the earlier estate hasn't been distributed yet.

Following are some specifics of why a will is needed.

- The will puts a structure in place, designating how, when and for what time frame income and asset distributions will be made, and to whom; and the person to perform each type of function, and who will invest the funds and actually make the distributions.

- A will provides the opportunity to designate a guardian for minor children. The testator usually has better insight than a court into which of their relatives or friends will best be able to care for their children, both emotionally and financially.

- The will can also provide for payments to the guardian to defray additional costs for caring for the children. If there is no will and if the children are minors, it will be necessary for the person who is to care for the children to apply to a court for permission to so do, and for any funding that would be needed. The court will also require a fiduciary (e.g., a trustee) to be appointed to receive and manage the property the children inherit. This can be a cumbersome and expensive process, requiring court supervision throughout the children's minority. The will can designate the trustee of the funds set aside for the children and guardians and provide instructions of what can be distributed to the guardian.

- A will provides the ability to leave assets in trusts with the income going to one set of beneficiaries or the spouse while the principal will go to others. The terms and timing of principal distributions can also be set in a will, which cannot be done if there is no will. The distributions in accordance with a will can be unequal and based on need among the group of beneficiaries or based on the discretion of the executor or trustee appointed in the will, while distributions where there is no will have to be applied for to the court and explained why they are needed.

- A will permits specific assets or amounts to be designated for certain people, who are not necessarily family members.

- A will provides for distributions to charitable organizations and possibly under what conditions. The will can also designate family foundations to be the inheritor of the charitable bequests, and this cannot be done without a will.

- You can use a will to disinherit someone or specifically exclude someone from inheriting anything from you. With no will, this person might be entitled to a share of the net estate assets.

- A will also can simplify the probate process for survivors. For example, a will designates a personal representative also known as an executor to handle the estate and wind down the decedent's affairs.

- The will can direct how taxes and debts should be paid, and can call for the waiving of bonding requirements for executors and trustees and state limitations on types of investments or payments.

- The will can also facilitate and enable an estate to take maximum advantage of estate tax savings.

- A will sets the stage for executors to ease the distribution of assets to trusts and beneficiaries named in the will and for the choice of assets.

WHAT HAPPENS IF YOU HAVE A WILL . . .

If you prepared a will	Your family has to find it. Where did you put it? It should be in a designated location.	If you have minor children—did you name who the guardian would be? If the other parent of the children is living, then your designation is not effective. If the other parent is not living, then the will of the second to die prevails.	Does the will say who pays the estate tax on assets passing outside of the estate? (IRAs, pensions, life insurance are examples of assets passing outside of the estate)	Did you forget to name someone that should have been mentioned in the will such as a child born out of wedlock, or from a previous marriage, or a child of a deceased child? Or a long term care giver? Does the will say who gets inheritances from you for heirs that die in a common disaster with you?
		If you did not designate a guardian you are no better off than if you had no will with regard to who will be taking care of your children.		
		If you did not provide for payments to the guardian you will cause the guardian to go to court to get payments when they are needed.		

WHAT HAPPENS IF YOU DON'T HAVE A WILL . . .

If you did not have a will.	Your family will waste a lot of time looking for it and then discussing how stupid you were by not having one.	State law will determine who gets what and when after some legal proceedings. State law will say who takes care of your children if there are no surviving parents. The person who wants to be the guardian will have to engage an attorney, go to court and have a judge decide. If there are two people who want to be the guardian, a judge will decide who they think is better to do it. Also, the guardian will have to apply to the court anytime they need funds to be used for the child's or children's support, education and well being.	State law will determine who will pay the estate tax (usually it will be apportioned over everyone who receives anything that would be included on the estate tax return). Estate taxes, if applicable, will usually be higher. Also, you cannot leave anything in trust with "strings attached." If a beneficiary is a minor, the court will determine when they will be entitled to receive any distributions at all and when the entire remaining amount would be distributed.	People that you might not want to leave anything to might be entitled by law to receive part of your assets. Nothing can be given to charity.

Chapter 4

Your Other "Wills"

The will is the main document for an estate plan and the planning leading to the execution of the will is quite extensive. However, the will is not the only document that determines how a decedent's assets are to be distributed.

Keep in mind that irrespective of whether assets pass through a will or outside of the will, assets owned by the decedent will be included in the gross assets for estate tax purposes.

Will substitutes

Designation forms are a will substitute for all accounts where they are used or provided for with default provisions. Distributions from beneficiary designated accounts are not determined by the will (unless the estate is the beneficiary which is a no no in most situations); do not pass through the estate; are not subject to the probate process; and are out of the control of the executor. However, they are considered to be estate taxable assets since they were assets of the deceased when he died.

Separately designated beneficiary designations

Not included in the will are assets that are designated separately how they are to be distributed upon death. These are the designation of beneficiary forms that are filled out with respect to many types of assets. These include pension, 401k, 403b and IRA plans, life and accident insurance policies, brokerage and bank accounts, Certificates of Deposit ("CD's"), mutual funds and variable and fixed annuities.

Certain types of accounts will pass outside of the estate even if there are no named beneficiaries. These include many pension, 401k, 403b and IRA accounts that have default beneficiaries that are not the estate such as the account owner's spouse.

Accounts naming a joint owner or a person payable on death

Distributions from accounts that name beneficiaries, or that have default beneficiaries, are not determined by the will (unless the estate is the beneficiary). Such accounts are considered to be estate taxable assets, but their distribution and administration do not pass through the estate and are not subject to the probate process, and are out of the control of the executor. The designation forms are a will substitute for all such accounts.

Distributions to spouses are not subject to estate tax. However, an estate tax can result for beneficiaries other than a spouse. Additionally, if the will is improperly drawn, the estate taxes on those amounts could reduce amounts that are intended to pass tax-free to a spouse, thus causing additional estate taxes on the estate taxes! This can occur where the residuary (assets left after all specific bequests) estate is solely responsible to pay debts of the decedent and the estate taxes. This can be avoided if the will provides for apportionment for each person inheriting assets that are subject to estate taxes to pay their share of the taxes.

The applicability of apportionment for you is something that should be explained to you by your advisor or attorney. Simply put, estate taxes can be paid either fully by the estate, or allocated or apportioned among everyone inheriting assets that will be subject to estate taxes. Apportionment will reduce the inheritances of those receiving specific or designated amounts or assets, while having the estate pay the taxes will reduce the inheritance of the person you want to leave everything left over to (called the residuary estate). Either way, the inheritances are reduced by estate taxes. Apportionment allows you to designate whose inheritance is reduced.

Jointly owned property

Jointly owned property and property owned by a trust or through a power of appointment are also assets that do not pass through the will.

CHAPTER 5

FORMS OF OWNERSHIP

Following is a listing of some types of ownership.

Type of account or designation	Description
Joint tenancy or joint tenancy with rights of survivorship	This is a form of joint ownership where all joint owners have an undivided interest in the entire property. If one joint owner dies, the others become the complete owners of the property. The last survivor gets the entire property.
Tenancy by the entirety	Form of ownership limited to a husband and wife in which each has an undivided interest in the entire property. The survivor ends up with the entire property.
Tenancy in common	Form of joint ownership where each party owns a specified share of the property. There is no right of survivorship. When one owner dies, their share goes to their estate (or a beneficiary that is designated), not to the other owner.
Community property	This is limited to married couples in the states of Arizona, California, Idaho, Louisiana, Nevada, New Mexico, Texas, Washington and Wisconsin. The assets included are all property acquired during the marriage while they are domiciled in a community property state, except property received as a gift or inheritance. Each spouse is deemed to own half of the property.
Custodian for a minor	Under state Uniform Gifts (or Transfers) to Minor Acts ("UGMA") an adult person can hold title to property for the benefit of a minor. Upon the minor reaching majority, the funds must be transferred to the minor's name. Assets held under UGMA use the social security number of the minor and the income is reported on the minors tax return.

Trusteeship	Assets held in a trust are "owned" by the Trustee for the benefit of the Trust beneficiaries as designed in the Trust agreement. There are many different types of trusts and many different ways they are formed. A trust formed by a person is considered an Inter Vivos Trust. A trust formed under a will is called a Testamentary Trust.
Totten Trust	This is not actually a trust but a designation on an account at a financial institution where someone other than the depositor or account owner is named as a beneficiary in the event of the owner's death. The designation would have the owner's name with "in trust for _____ [beneficiary's name]" after it. Upon the owner's death, title immediately transfers to the "in trust for" person.

CHAPTER 6

ASSETS INCLUDED IN AN ESTATE

When someone dies, their heirs or executors have to account for all of their assets. The range of assets included in an estate is quite broad. Following are some types of assets included in an estate.

- Everything the decedent owned outright

- Everything the decedent owned as a tenant in common

- Everything the decedent owned with someone else where they had the right of survivorship, except for the other person's portion to the extent they contributed to its purchase or acquisition

- Life insurance proceeds where the ownership of the policy is attributed to decedent

- Life insurance policies transferred by decedent within three years of death

- IRAs, 401k, 403b, Roth IRAs, Roth 401k's, pensions and other deferred plans

- Powers of appointment where decedent could have appointed himself

- Everything in Qualified Terminal Interest Property ("QTIP") trusts where decedent was the beneficiary

- Accounts where decedent was the custodian for a grandchild and where decedent contributed the principal to the account

- Gift taxes paid by decedent within three years of their death

Assets people don't know they have

Many times there have to be searches or investigations for assets the decedent may not have even known he had. Following are some items that should be looked for:

- "Abandoned" life insurance where there was a permanent portion that was paid up insurance

- Life insurance policies issued as a "come on" by banks and credit card companies. Many banks send you a policy for $1,000 with no charge and ask you to sign up for more insurance whose premiums will be billed to your credit cards or account monthly. These $1,000 policies should be searched for and enquiries should be made to the banks where decedent maintained an account

- Look at all credit card and bank charges for the last three years to see if any life insurance policies have been paid for by charges to the accounts

- Mortgage life insurance

- Insurance on credit card debt and auto loans and consumer credit loans

- Look for safe deposit boxes. Search checking accounts for the last five years for checks made out to banks and find out what they were for

- Investigate all checks and credit card charges for the last five years to determine if any assets were purchased that are unaccounted for. You can investigate some of these by following through with whoever endorsed the checks

- Follow up on all transfers and withdrawals from brokerage accounts for the last five years to trace the destination of the transfers

- Look at telephone bills for the last three years to see if the identity of the receiver of any repetitive phone calls is known. Sometimes frequent calls could have been made to a brokerage firm where the statements were sent to the deceased at a different location such as their office

- UCC searches can be done to see if there are any liens filed on assets that are not included in the estate listing

- Review the decedent's tax returns for the last five years to see if there have been any major drops in income that are not accounted for; if all the income is matched with assets that are included in the estate listing; and if anything else is indicated on the return that should be looked at further

- Review insurance policies for the last five years, if available, to see that all insured property is identified on the asset list

- If decedent owned a business or interests in a business, review the distributions from the business for the last few years to see if any distributions have been diverted in any manner to acquire assets that should be included in the estate

Performing these searches are necessary and could be tedious, costly and time consuming. This is a reason for things to be in order or for a trail to be left so that settling the estate can be done in an expeditious manner.

How assets are valued in an estate

Assets are valued for estate tax purposes at the full value the moment before death or in some circumstances, the value six months later (called the alternate valuation date).

The alternate valuation date has to be specifically elected. Making this election depends on the amounts subject to estate taxes, the degree of changes between the two dates, the probable tax situation of the beneficiaries inheriting the assets and what the beneficiaries will be doing with the assets, such as selling, retaining and if retained, whether it will be available for depreciation deductions.

CHAPTER 7

ESTATE LIQUIDITY

Many times an estate does not have sufficient liquid assets to provide a source of current funds to the heirs and/or to pay the estate taxes. Please note that in most situations the estate taxes are due nine months after death. Selling illiquid assets can take longer than that.

Many people have much of their wealth in illiquid assets such as real estate or closely held family businesses. Others have young families and simply do not have available cash; while some have liquid stocks and bond portfolios that are not able to be appropriately sold if there is a drastic event that causes a huge drop in market values or market liquidity; while still others have plenty of cash but in accounts not readily accessible by the survivors needing to use the cash to maintain their current lifestyle. Another situation for liquidity is where there is an untimely death of both parents leaving young children to the care of a guardian that will need financial assistance almost from day one.

A reasonable way to handle this is to set up a bank account with an adequate[1] balance that is in joint name with a spouse, or a second person, that will need the cash availability in the event of a death. The second person on the account does not have to have ready access to the account during the settlor's lifetime, and simply has to sign the account papers and signature cards and be told the location of the checkbooks should they be needed.

Another method of dealing with the liquidity issue is for the decedent to have life insurance payable to the heirs, either directly, or through an irrevocable trust (see

---

[1] The amount comprising "adequate" will depend on each individual situation and the guessed at period the immediate needs will be for. An example is to have available cash to cover six months or one year's expenses.

next section). This can present a relatively low-cost solution while the estate is being probated or the estate plan formulated. In the event that there are sufficient liquid assets to cover taxes, costs and other items, then, obviously, this is not an issue.

It is suggested that a careful listing of what would become estate assets be made and examined considering the liquidity issue.

CHAPTER 8

LIFE INSURANCE

Life insurance can be an effective vehicle for providing liquidity, increasing an estate and providing for payment of estate taxes.

There are many different types of policies, as reasons to purchase or invest in them, and wide ranges of costs for the same death benefits. This is not covered here with the reader advised to seek the counsel of a professional life insurance agent who could provide alternate policy costs, benefits and detriments of the various choices needed to be made. You should also consider a consultation with your CPA or financial planner to determine your needs and whether the proposals adequately address those needs.

Note that any life insurance policy owed by the deceased or any policy that they had any control over is called "incidents of ownership" and will be included in their taxable estate no matter who the beneficiary is.

Life insurance should not be owned by insured

It is inadvisable for life insurance to be owned by, or attributed to, the insured and in many cases, by their spouse. This is because life insurance proceeds from any policy controlled in any manner by the insured will be included in their estate. If the spouse is the beneficiary, there will be no estate tax until the spouse passes away while still retaining some of the funds. If the spouse dies simultaneous with the insured, then the proceeds will be included in the estate and taxed accordingly.

Life insurance should be owned by an irrevocable trust (preferred by the author) or by the beneficiaries (not a preferred method). See next chapter for the way to set up an insurance trust. I don't recommend the children owning the policy because creditors of that child might have claims against the policy (if there is cash value) or against the proceeds after the death of the insured. Also the proceeds will become part of their assets and can end up outside of the family bloodline if that person dies and leaves all their assets to their spouse who in turn will leave their money to a subsequent spouse. Trusts eliminate these eventualities and can also keep the funds permanently free from estate taxation.

CHAPTER 9

IRREVOCABLE LIFE INSURANCE TRUST

The following are the steps that should be followed to set up an irrevocable life insurance trust and to remove all incidents of ownership from an insured.

1. Create an Irrevocable Life Insurance Trust ("ILIT") to assume outright ownership and all incidents of ownership of all the policies. This is a legal document that needs to be prepared by an attorney.

2. You will need to name a trustee and alternate trustee to administer over the trust. It is not suggested you name people that can benefit from the trust's assets.

3. The trust will become the sole beneficiary of any life insurance policies owned by the trust.

4. You will need to name beneficiaries to receive any income earned by the trust and/or principal in the trust. An example is for your spouse to be the income beneficiary and your children, principal beneficiaries. The trust can also state how long the income payments will continue and under what circumstances.

5. The trustee should be given the right to invade principal for ascertainable standards of health and welfare of your spouse, children, or other beneficiaries.

6. You can also give the trustee the right to invade principal and distribute funds to the beneficiaries for any reason they feel necessary and appropriate under the then current situations.

7. You can also give the trustee the right to distribute income, or principal, disproportionately based on need, or individual circumstances as they arise.

8. The trust can provide that the children and/or other beneficiaries will receive a pro rata share of the total trust assets when they reach a certain age or stage in their lives. An example is 1/3 upon reaching age 25, 1/2 of the remaining balance upon attaining age 30, and the balance at age 35. Alternatively, the trust can provide that a portion be distributed upon attaining significant events in their lives including marriage, receiving certain college or university degrees or honorable discharge from the armed forces.

9. The transfer of all incidents of ownership of existing policies to the trust might result in the creation of a taxable gift. To the extent thereof, a gift tax return will have to be filed and either a gift tax paid or the lifetime exemption applied. It can also be arranged for the gifts to be done in stages.

10. To the extent premiums would be due, annual gifts could be made to the trust. If annual gifts are made, then "Crummey Letters" (see next chapter) should be prepared to permit the allowance of annual gift tax exclusions for the premiums so that those amounts will not be considered as taxable gifts.

11. If grandchildren can become recipients of the life insurance, there will be generation shipping transfer issues which are not covered in here. You are cautioned to seek competent advice in that regard.

12. If the insured dies within three years of moving an existing policy to the trust, the proceeds would still be includible in their estate. This applies to presently existing policies either under direct ownership or a company's.

13. If new or additional insurance is purchased, it should be acquired directly by the trust. The three-year rule does not apply to policies purchased directly by the trust.

14. Irrevocable life insurance trust assets and insurance proceeds are excluded from estates and estate taxation. Proceeds received after death that include interest or other ordinary income will be subject to income tax by the trust.

15. If the trust has income (such as interest, dividends or capital gains) during the lifetime of the grantor, the income will be taxed on the grantor's individual income tax return. This is subject to "grantor trust" rules.

16. The trust is a legal entity under the law. However during the lifetime of the grantor, no separate taxpayer identification number needs to be applied for—the grantor's Social Security number can be used and no separate tax returns need to be filed by the trust. After the death of the grantor, separate identification numbers then have to be obtained and tax returns filed.

17. Note that life insurance owned by an insured where their divorced spouse is a beneficiary will be included in the insured's estate while the divorced spouse receives all or some of the death benefit (and the insured's estate will be subject to pay the estate tax on those funds). Irrevocable life insurance trusts owning the policies avoid these types of problems. Also a will's apportionment clause can possibly reduce some of the taxes paid by the estate.

CHAPTER 10

CRUMMEY LETTER

Annual gift tax exclusions are available for gifts of present interests. Usually a gift made to an irrevocable life insurance trust is not considered a gift of a present interest and is not subject to the annual exclusion. However, such gifts can be made eligible for the exclusion by providing the beneficiary with a "Crummey Letter" giving the beneficiary the right to withdraw their portion of the money for a limited period. Crummey is the name based on the court case the taxpayer won.

If the donee does not waive their rights to their portion of the gift, then that amount of the gift will be subject to gift tax by the donor. Accordingly, it is important for the donee to waive their rights. If they elect to take a distribution then the funds will not be available to pay the insurance premiums and this will raise other problems and issues (not covered here).

It is suggested that the following steps be followed:

1. The trustee opens a bank account with minimal funds provided by the grantor in the trust's name using the grantor's Social Security number. Those funds from the grantor are considered as a gift.

2. Thirty days before the premiums are due the grantor should make a gift of that amount to the trust.

3. Immediately upon depositing the funds, the trustee should give each beneficiary a Crummey Letter where they have the right to withdraw those funds, or where they waive their right to withdraw those funds deposited in the trust. Each beneficiary will get a letter for their proportionate amount of the gift.

4. After the thirty day period expires, or signed letters are received earlier by the trustee, the trustee should pay the premium, making sure that it is not paid late. If there is no response by the beneficiary it should be assumed they waived their right to a distribution.

On the following page is a sample Crummey Letter. It is cautioned that an attorney be consulted to prepare a sample Crummey Letter in accordance with the terms of the trust and the current tax laws.

SAMPLE CRUMMEY LETTER

_____ Trust U/A/D _____

_____, Trustee

_____

_____

Date:_____

_____

_____

_____

Re: Trust Withdrawal Rights

Dear_____,

As you may know, your _____ (grandparents) (parents) have created a trust, entitled as stated on the top line of this letter, naming you as a beneficiary.

Under the trust, you are entitled to withdraw on an annual basis the lessor of $_____ or the amount actually contributed to the trust for your benefit. This year, your withdrawal amount is $_____. The Trust Agreement gives you the unrestricted right to withdraw such part or all of this amount, as you wish, to use for your own uses and purposes.

If you wish to exercise the withdrawal rights conferred upon you, you must do so within <u>thirty (30) days</u> from the date of this letter. Please check box below and sign where indicated.

If you do not intend to exercise the withdrawal rights granted to you, please so indicate by checking box and signing below. *If there is no response, it will signify that you waived your right to a withdrawal.*

Should you have any questions, please do not hesitate to contact me.

Cordially yours,

_____, Trustee

☐ I acknowledge receipt of this notice to withdraw cash transferred to the Trust <u>and</u> <u>wish to withdraw $</u>_____.

_____
Signature

☐ I acknowledge receipt of this notice to withdraw property transferred to the Trust, <u>but decline to do so.</u>

_____
Signature

CHAPTER 11

TRUSTS

Trusts are not necessary in most estate plans, but when they are used properly, they provide significant benefits.

Many trusts provide a means of distributing income and principal in an orderly managed way. Some trusts provide a degree of asset protection, designate a group or class of beneficiaries, and force the use of professional financial planners, managers and trustees. Some trusts are set up to outlive the presently living beneficiaries and need to have appropriate protections and guarantees. And some trusts are set up to avoid or circumvent the probate process.

Definition of a trust

A trust is an entity established by a person, called a grantor, for the benefit of others, called beneficiaries, that is controlled or operated by a third person or entity called a trustee.

The beneficiaries can consist of one group that receives the current income or fixed dollar amount or percentage or assets and another group who will receive the trust principal or corpus at a later time. The principal beneficiaries can also be the same people as the income beneficiaries. The beneficiaries can also be people not living yet, such as children born after the trust is established. There is wide flexibility and great leeway in setting up who the beneficiaries are and the distribution terms, but once established, they cannot easily be changed if at all.

Trustees and their powers

Trustees can be individuals, or entities such as a bank or trust company. There can be a single trustee or multiple trustees. Trustees have very broad powers to not only control the distributions in amount and timing and sometimes to whom, but also how to invest the principal. Trustees can also have broad powers to invade principal to make a distribution to a particular beneficiary to exclusion of other beneficiaries.

All powers given to trustees are explained and detailed in the trust document. Any power not given in the trust agreement cannot be done, with certain narrow exceptions.

How trusts are established

Trusts can either be established by someone that is living or through a will. Trusts are formed under the laws of the jurisdiction where they are set up. The different states have their own rules, as do foreign countries. Some states and countries are particularly useful in creating trusts for specific purposes. When establishing a trust it is necessary to use an attorney familiar with the different jurisdictions and purposes for that particular trust.

Trusts set up during the lifetime of the grantor are called inter vivos trusts. Trusts that are established pursuant to a will are referred to as testamentary trusts. Trusts can be set up as a separate document or within a will or other trust. Trusts set up in a will have no meaning and have no effect until the testator dies, and the will is probated.

Irrevocable trusts

Trusts where absolute title to assets transferred to the trust passes to the trust with an independent trustee are irrevocable. Lifetime (inter vivos) transfers made to an irrevocable trust are subject to gift tax.

Trusts where the grantor can make changes whenever they want for whatever purposes are revocable.

Grantor trusts

This is a type of trust that is irrevocable and where the grantor is not the trustee but has certain rights as defined in Internal Revenue Code ("IRC") Sections 671—679.

Because of these rights the trust's income is reported on the grantor's individual income tax return and the grantor pays the income tax instead of the trust or beneficiaries that receive income or income distributions. The grantor pays the tax regardless of whether he receives any income or distributions from the trust. Inter vivos transfers to grantor trusts are subject to gift taxes the same as for non grantor trusts.

A common grantor trust is an irrevocable life insurance trust as described in a separate chapter. Gifts to the trust are taxable gifts and the life insurance is not included in the estate of the grantor, but any income earned by the trust during the lifetime of the grantor is included in the grantor's individual tax return.

Separate taxpayer identification numbers ("TIN") are not required—the grantor's Social Security number is used. Some banks, brokers and insurance companies require the separate TINs, causing fiduciary tax returns to be filed, but the income is still taxed by the grantor.

Sometimes grantor trusts are called defective trusts because they violate "sound" trust drafting rules that cause them to fall under the IRC §671-679 traps set up to "catch you." They are "defective" based on tax laws. Using grantor or defective trusts can be a sound estate planning tool and are perfectly legal if used in the proper circumstances.

Living trusts

A trust set up by a grantor where they are the trustee is called a living trust. Living trusts are always revocable, and are not recognized for income or estate tax purposes. Transfers to a living trust are not subject to gift taxes.

Living trusts become irrevocable upon death of the grantor/trustee. At that point, the alternate trustee immediately becomes the trustee and assumes complete control of the trust.

Living trusts are occasionally considered and used as substitute wills, but should not negate preparing a standard will.

Living trusts do not need to file tax returns, or use taxpayer identification numbers. They use the grantor's Social Security number and the transactions are reported on the grantor's individual income tax return. All transactions in the living trust are disregarded for any tax purposes—income and estate.

See separate chapter on living trusts.

Some trust benefits and costs

A trust will possibly provide for a degree of asset protection and a shield from future creditors. This is a very technical issue and should not be used for asset protection purposes without a serious consultation with an experienced attorney in that area of law.

Dynasty trusts can be set up to last past the lives of children and grandchildren, and those yet to be born. A trust can designate almost any distribution terms and conditions as to both to the income beneficiary and to the principal beneficiary.

Be aware that costs will be incurred in establishing the trust and in trust maintenance, operation, government reporting and tax return filing.

Trusts for minor children

See separate chapter on ways to leave assets to minors.

CHAPTER 12

TOTAL RETURN TRUSTS

When trust provisions call for all income to be distributed to a beneficiary or class of beneficiaries, then the only amounts that can be distributed is the actual income.[2] In many situations there is an inequity in the way the assets are invested as compared to the desires of either the income or principal beneficiaries. This conflict is handled by some state "total return" trust laws.

Total return trusts ("TRT") are not specific trusts but are elections that trusts make to have distributions of trust income and principal made in different amounts or percentages than actual income. These elections are made under state laws and supersede directions incorporated in the agreement establishing the trust, but can also be established in the trust.

Even though each state's laws are different, the concepts, planning, principles and workings are substantially the same, so this discussion will not differentiate between individual states. Those contemplating the possibilities of TRT elections are cautioned and directed to seek legal counsel in the state they or the trust is domiciled and in states where their will might also have to be probated.

How TRTs work

The trustee would make an election to have TRT provisions implemented. Beneficiaries may have a right to contest.

---

2   State laws might define a trust's income differently than the taxable or annual income usually associated with investments. An executor or trustee should become familiar with this terminology and the amounts they can legally distribute.

The TRT provides a "guaranteed" distribution to income beneficiaries regardless of actual income. Distributions are made based on the value of trust assets. There are exclusions for assets used by the beneficiary such as rent-free occupancy of a residence.

Why TRTs

No matter who the grantor is, or how their family and beneficiaries are constituted there is a divergence of interests between the current income beneficiary and ultimate principal beneficiary.

- The income beneficiary would want as much income as possible.
- The principal beneficiary would want to eventually inherit as much as possible.

What TRTs do

TRTs recognize that there are different interests in a trust; that inflation that will erode the value of a fixed income portfolio; and that there are many ways of prudent investing that do not necessarily provide high income on a short-term basis.

- TRTs recognize that many trusts have provided for "all income" to spouse (or other beneficiaries) without providing for changing investing patterns, styles or needs or changes in the economy.

- TRTs permit any type of "prudent" investing as long as minimum distributions are provided to the "income" beneficiaries.

- TRT laws have been enacted to permit a balance between the current interests of the income beneficiaries and the long-term residual interests of the corpus beneficiaries.

- TRTs permit fixed annual (or monthly or quarterly) distributions to the income beneficiary that is in excess of actual current income. This permits a reduction of principal or the payment of capital gains if necessary to pay the fixed amount.

Edward Mendlowitz, CPA

- The asset values will have to be reevaluated annually to determine the amount the TRT percentage will be applied against.

Example
Assume the actual income is 2% on a $2,000,000 portfolio totally invested in stocks, and that all the income is to be distributed annually to the widow(er).

Without TRT laws, the widow(er) may not be receiving an adequate return and can petition to have the assets reinvested to provide greater current income.

With a 4% TRT, $80,000 will be paid annually, instead of just the $40,000 income. $40,000 will come from income and $40,000 from principal.

A TRT invested solely in stocks might not be considered prudent but any increases in the value of the stocks will inure to the eventual benefit of the principal or corpus beneficiary. Likewise, a portfolio invested in long-term high yield bonds would provide very high income but would subject the principal to risk and no growth.

- TRTs recognize changing situations or that there will be changing situations and permit the trustees to decide on the proper investment balance in reaction to the changes.

- TRTs allow the trustees to invest with the interests of the corpus beneficiaries better balanced with the interests of the current income beneficiaries.

- TRTs remove pressure on the trustee to make investments placing a greater importance on either the current income beneficiaries or the corpus beneficiaries.

See chapter on trustees' investment responsibilities

CHAPTER 13

CHOOSING EXECUTORS AND TRUSTEES

Executors

An Executor or Personal Representative has to be selected. The duties of the Executor, or Executrix if a woman, is to marshal the assets, pay the estate's liabilities including taxes, and turn the remaining assets over to the beneficiaries.

Probate is the process of doing this, and it is usually done under the supervision of a probate or surrogates court (or other appropriate jurisdiction).

Settling an estate is a process that could take some time—a few months to a few years depending upon the complexity of the Estate, speed at which the Executors work and responsiveness of third parties involved (such as banks and brokers, general partners, children and other relatives). During this period, the Executors have complete control of the estate's affairs and assets.

Trustees

To the extent there are trusts, trustees will have to be chosen. Different people from the executors are occasionally chosen conferring different rights and obligations to the Executors and Trustees. The Trustees do not assume their duties until the assets are distributed to them.

In some respect, the choice of trustees is a more important decision than choosing an Executor since, once the estate is settled the Executor's job is completed. The Trustees, however, will remain until all the assets are ultimately distributed.

The testator or grantor should select Trustees whom they believe will exercise strong, fair, compassionate and independent judgment.

Some suggestions of who can be considered as Trustees are a bank, attorney, accountant, spouse, close friend, cousin, nephew or similar type of relative. It is also important that whomever is chosen be fiscally astute and that the spouse and\or other primary beneficiaries have comfort in the selection. Further, a group can be designated that can provide for divergent interests to be represented. If an odd number is selected there will be a built in mechanism for tie breaking.

Executors' and Trustees' fees

All executors and trustees are entitled to statutory fees, and if nothing is said, this will automatically apply. If there is a desire to not pay fees, it should be specifically stated.

Bonding

Executors and trustees may or may not be bonded and this will be determined by what the will or trust provides for this. Bonds are obtained from insurance companies and assure the proper performance of the executor and trustee.

I have seen a situation where a daughter applied to the Surrogate's Court to be the administrator of her father's estate when he died without a will; and the bonding company would not issue a bond at a standard fee because of her irresponsible credit history. None of the other siblings wanted to assume that responsibility so the cost to the estate was much greater and there was a six-week delay in having her appointed by the court. The legal fees in that regard were also higher because of the added meetings, discussions and motions.

CHAPTER 14

TRUSTEES' INVESTMENT RESPONSIBILITIES

Most trustees have inherent and serious conflicts on how to invest the assets. Besides individual investment decisions and deciding on an overall big picture asset allocation plan, trustees need to balance the interests of the income and corpus beneficiaries.

Trustees need to decide whether to invest the funds to maximize current income, or to provide for either the safety or growth, or both, of the ultimate principal. In many cases it is a massive guessing game with the conflicting parties wanting what appears best for them at that time. Further as with most investment decisions, it is a moving target with many outside influences affecting what has to be done.

How a trustee invests the funds is a very real issue that many times is not confronted until the trustee is performing their job and one group of beneficiaries criticizes the results. Here are some typical questions that arise.

Question 1: Assume a spouse aged 75 is income beneficiary and his or her children aged around 50 are principal beneficiaries. How should the trust assets be invested? For high current income or to preserve or grow capital?

Comment: Does it really matter? Probably not. The trustee will invest in a manner that will provide reasonable income while maintaining asset security and as close to market-based growth as makes sense.

Question 2: Now consider the same question but the spouse is a second spouse (with their own children) and is about 10 years older than the oldest child who is the principal beneficiary. Does it matter?

Comment: You bet it does. The second spouse would most likely prefer the income to be as high as possible since any money they receive that is not used will be left to accumulate for their children. The principal beneficiaries of the trust would usually prefer that the principal be invested to grow as much as possible with current income not being the concern. Now assume the trustee is independent and aware of both groups concerns. A compromise plan would be to invest the assets half in fixed income (with higher current yields but little or no potential for growth) and half in equities (with lower current yields but high potential for growth). Now, lets make everyone 10 years younger. The surviving spouse is about 50 and children about 40. Why wouldn't the surviving spouse want higher growth potential built into a portfolio that might provide them with income for 40 or more years? Would a 50-50 split accomplish this, or would a 70-30 split weighted toward equities be the more appropriate way to invest?

Question 3:   What would a testator prefer, or suggest, or "dictate" from the grave? Could that be written into the will or trust? Assuming so, would that be the same today as it would have been ten years ago? __Yes __No

Comment: Probably not! Just look how Treasury yields or 5 year CD rates have changed from 10 years ago. Also, look how the S&P 500 has performed, with dividends over the same period. Compare that to the previous ten-year period. Completely different.

Question 4:   How concerned should the trustee be about safety of the portfolio?

Comment: Probably very concerned. Since late 2008 through 2011 there has been a flight to safety such as never seen before. Also, safety takes many forms. Is a 20 year Treasury bond safer than a 1 year bank CD; or a 20 year AAA Corporate bond safer than a 5 year "junk" bond?

Example 1:   Assume a 20 year corporate bond portfolio will yield 5% and 1 year bank CDs yield 1.25%. If the trustee wants to maximize income without any "risk" would they would buy the 20 year bonds or the 1 year CDs?

Now assume it is three years later and the income beneficiary dies and the 17-year market yields increased to 7% causing the principal to decline in value 25%. What would your answer to the previous question have been?

Example 2: Use the same rates as previous example. The trustee wants to maximize principal security and value, so they buy the CDs. It is twenty years later and the income beneficiary is still alive. The cumulative inflation has been 60% (what it has been for the past 20 years) and the income no longer provides for the needs of the income beneficiary. Further, the principal beneficiary can look forward to eventually inheriting assets with at least a 60% decreased buying power. How can the trustee explain their actions? How much weight should be given to inflation? FYI, inflation over the last ten years was about 28%, and 60% over the last twenty years. Further, does inflation have as much effect on an 80 year old as it does on a 40 year old?

Example 3. The trustee anticipates the income beneficiary having a long healthy life and wants to invest 60% in the stock market and 40% in long term bonds. The anticipated income is 2% on the stocks and 4.5% on the bonds. The portfolio yield would be 3% (60% x 2% plus 40% x 4.5%). This is a compromise position possibly not completely satisfying either or one set of beneficiaries. Is this a reasonable approach? Now suppose the income beneficiary dies prematurely. Which example would you want followed?

Question 5: What are the typical conventional investment choices a trustee has?

Comment: The most conventional choices are stocks, bonds and CDs. The stocks and bonds could be purchased individually, in mutual funds or in index or exchange traded funds. Following are broad-based allocation positions.

- All long term bonds
- All short term CDs or bonds
- All stocks
- Balanced between some CDs, bonds and stocks

Note that each choice has many variations—such as the stocks could be small, mid or large cap growth or value (that's six choices), could spread among U.S. foreign and emerging markets (that increases the choices to 18). Now factor in the choices of individual securities or mutual funds, or engaging an investment manager charging an annual fee. These are not so simple, but are real decisions that are made daily by trustees.

Edward Mendlowitz, CPA

Question 6:   What happens when the trustee is someone completely trusted by the testator or grantor but who does not have a reasonable level of financial sophistication?

Comment: The trustee will be the heirs' decision maker. Many people try to choose trustees that they trust, with that confidence extending to the belief the trustee will seek professional guidance for investing decisions, asset allocation, asset management and selection, rebalancing, and financial crisis management. For the nonfinancial issues, they should want a trustee that would be a sympathetic, available, reasonable, fair and kind ear if a beneficiary needs a current distribution of principal.

CHAPTER 15

LIVING TRUSTS

Many people deem it necessary or propitious to transfer their assets while they are living to a revocable trust (called a Living Trust).

A living trust is a method that avoids or eliminates much of the probate process. It does not save taxes—either income or estate taxes—but it can facilitate many of the decisions and actions that need to take place after a person's death. Living trusts are much more appropriate in certain states than others. Attorneys in a given state can advise on this.

In a living trust, the grantor would be the trustee and the ultimate trustee would be the alternate. Upon the grantor's death, the alternate trustee would immediately assume control of the trust's assets, completely bypassing the probate process.

A business, partnership units, or certain types of investment property are the type of assets that should be considered for a living trust. This would enable the reins to be transferred instantly upon the death of the grantor, without any delay or waiting for the will to be probated. This could be especially important if there is a potential sale or important contract negotiation in process.

When a living trust is established substantially all of a person's assets or those assets that would most benefit from the trust such as a business or partnership interest should be transferred to the trust.

Please note that the IRS does not require that the living trust obtain a separate Federal identification number nor does it require separate annual tax returns during the grantor's lifetime. The grantor's Social Security number continues to be used.

Edward Mendlowitz, CPA

A tale of two estates

The following illustrates the advantages of leaving assets in a living trust rather than in your own name. This table is not complete and has been prepared to illustrate a comparison between the two alternatives. Looking below at the probate process for someone with a will can make anyone without a will imagine how much more difficult it will be for their heirs!

Note that living trusts facilitate much of the probate process, but in some probate easy states such as New Jersey, many of the reasons for living trusts are not valid. You should discuss with an attorney the pros and cons of establishing living trusts for such purposes.

Timeline	Living Trust	Assets in Name of Decedent
Date of death	Assets in the living trust immediately become under control of successor trustee	Will has to be filed for probate
About a week later	Federal I.D. # obtained and trust bank account opened	Attorney should be engaged
About another week later		Attorney prepares some paperwork to get will ready to be filed for probate
	As income checks are received they can be deposited into trust account and then disbursed to beneficiaries as soon as checks clear	As income checks are received they must be held until the letters testamentary are issued
	If any business actions need to be taken by the owner, the trustee will have full power to take such action	No business actions can be taken with respect to any assets or property until the executor is qualified
	If the terms of the trust permit, the trust assets can be distributed to the beneficiaries. *Note that the estate might be taxed on the trust assets and the estate tax might have to be paid to the estate by the trust (or by the beneficiaries if the assets were distributed). Because of this it would be propitious for the trustee to hold back sufficient funds to cover the estate taxes, until the estate is settled*	Assets cannot be distributed to beneficiaries until letters testamentary are issued. At that time, some assets can be distributed to beneficiaries if it is clear who the beneficiaries will be. Enough assets should be withheld to make sure there would be funds to cover the estate taxes, pay liabilities and make distributions to other beneficiaries

About a month to three or four months later (if there are no problems). *Note that in some states this process takes much longer than others. New Jersey is a state with very favorable treatment of estates and the letters can be issued ten days after the date of death. New York is a medium difficult state, with certain counties such as Queens being particularly hard. Florida is a very difficult state for probate.*		Will filed and letters testamentary issued
About a few days afterwards		Federal I.D. # obtained and estate bank account opened
About six or seven months later (hopefully) or much later if there are problems or unforeseen issues.		Administrative or probate estate is settled (assuming no complications) and estate can disburse all remaining assets to beneficiaries
	Details of the trust's transactions and activities will be kept private. In general, nothing will have to be filed with the court. This could be very important if there is a special needs beneficiary or a child that is disinherited and it is desired for that information to remain private.	Details of the estate will become public information.
	The trust will generally have to report its transactions using a calendar year.	The estate can adopt a fiscal year that could possibly defer the taxation of the income.
	It is advisable for the income to be distributed rather than have the trust or estate pay the income tax since the trust or estate will usually be in a higher tax bracket than the income beneficiaries. Note that the income tax paid by the trust will be minimally higher than the income tax paid by the estate—the estate has a slightly larger exemption.	
Caution:	If it is possible that a beneficiary will disclaim any part of their inheritance, then absolutely no actions of any sort should be engaged in until that decision is made.	

CHAPTER 16

CREDIT SHELTER TRUST

A credit shelter trust ("CST") is any trust that receives the assets used to offset the estate tax exemption ($5,120,000 for 2012)[3] so that these assets avoid estate tax. CSTs are an alternative to leaving assets outright to a beneficiary. The lifetime estate tax exemption is sometimes referred to as the "credit shelter" amount.

Most of the time CST trusts are created in the will and do not become effective until the estate is settled and trust funded, but lifetime gifts can be made to an inter vivos CST if desired. CST provisions are also found in many living trusts that become activated upon the grantor's death.

When a credit shelter trust is used, typically the income will go to the surviving spouse and/or to other specific individuals, or can be allocated, i.e. sprinkled, among a group of beneficiaries that may or may not include the spouse. Sprinkled means the trustee has the power to distribute the income as they see fit among the class of beneficiaries.

Generally, the credit shelter trust is used to take advantage of the decedent's estate tax exemption but is also used by many others that do not have sufficient assets to pay estate taxes. Some of the reasons for credit shelter trusts are:

- To control the distribution of the income to a beneficiary or group of beneficiaries while the principal goes to another beneficiary or group of beneficiaries

- The assets will remain in a trust which would be protected from creditors

---

[3] The 2010 tax law established $5,000,000 for 2011 as the estate tax exemption amount to be adjusted annually for inflation. The inflation adjustment for 2012 was $120,000. This amount might be changed by legislation effective for 2013.

- Careful and deliberate planning with the trust investments and a selected distributions policy can provide for the growth of assets in the CST that will always be exempt from estate taxes

- Where the decedent's spouse has adequate income from other assets, distributions do not need to be made to the spouse allowing accumulation within the trust. Any amounts distributed to the spouse will possibly be subject to eventual estate taxes when they pass away

- The CST permits the first spouse to name the beneficiaries, not the surviving spouse

- The CST could have spendthrift provisions which will provide some asset protection for the beneficiaries

- The CST could have an independent trustee so that there could possibly be investment decision oversight and guidance

Portability

The 2010 tax law created portability of the lifetime exemption that permits unused lifetime exemptions of a spouse to be used by the estate of the second spouse to die.

At this writing, the lifetime exemption is $5,120,000 per person. Prior to portability careful planning was needed to assure that each spouse had sufficient assets in their separate name to make full use of the lifetime exemption. Portability is an essential tool for those without any plans or for those that stubbornly refuse to implement any planning because it enables the applying of two full lifetime exemptions or $10,240,000 regardless of how assets are titled.

Portability also comes into play where the first spouse to die leaves everything to their spouse not availing their estate of the $5.12 million exemption. Now, the estate of the second to die can use the full $10.24 million exemption. Under prior law, they would only be able to use their own $5.12 million exemption, wasting the opportunity to save estate tax on $5.12 million. Actually, proper planning under prior law in this situation would have had the first spouse to die leaving $5.12 million in a credit shelter trust where their spouse can get the income and if needed, principal distributions for rest of their life with the remaining or accumulated balance passing estate tax free to the next level of heirs.

Yet another way under prior law was disclaimer planning where the surviving spouse would disclaim up to $5.12 million of their inheritance in favor of the next tier of beneficiaries. This was sort of a default plan and was important with changing exemption amounts, but this required terms of a CST trust in the will.

Irrespective of the benefits of portability, the prior CST planning techniques are more preferable. First off, portability and other federal estate tax laws only apply to traditional spouses and not same sex marriage spouses. Secondly, CST planning presents many benefits portability does not as shown above. Thirdly, reconfiguration of assets remains an easy to do maneuver that allows the owner to make their own plans and protects against changing estate tax laws, except that this involves turning over ownership to a spouse that some may not want to do. Here are some specific reasons not to rely on portability.

- In order to use portability, a federal estate tax return must be filed even if not required, to make the election to apply the unused exemption to the estate of the second spouse to die.

- The portability election must be made, and if overlooked, it will be lost.

- The election will keep the statute of limitations on that return open until the exemption is utilized by the surviving spouse's estate perhaps giving the IRS an opportunity to look at certain valuations on the originally filed return. This would apply where the deceased spouse had some assets, but wasn't able to use the full exemption, or made prior gifts and did not file complete gift tax returns.

- If there is a subsequent remarriage and that new spouse dies then the transference of the unused exemption can only be done for the last deceased spouse, and not the earlier deceased spouse. This applies even if the estate of the last deceased spouse does not make the portability election. Note that portability is not automatic in the sense that it must be affirmatively elected. However, it is considered "automatic" in a negative sense if it is not elected in this situation.

- Portability applies to gift and estate taxes but not to generation skipping transfers.

- An overreliance on using portability might forestall CST planning in a currently drawn will, and if portability is not included in estate tax laws enacted for 2013 or later, the will could be inadequate and would need to be redone quickly.

- The unused portability exemption does not increase with inflation or due to growth in value or income on assets thereby freezing the unused exemption amount as of the date of death. Income on, and increases in the value of, assets placed in the CST will escape estate taxes when passed to the ultimate beneficiaries.

CHAPTER 17

QUALIFIED TERMINAL INTEREST PROPERTY ("QTIP") TRUST

I put the QTIP abbreviation in the heading because these trusts are universally referred to as QTIP trusts.

These are trusts where the surviving spouse gets the income and other beneficiaries the principal after the surviving spouse's death. Most of the time QTIP trusts are created in the will and do not become effective until the estate is settled and trust funded. They can also be established during lifetime, or through a living trust.

Many people leave most of their assets to their spouses, preferring to have the taxation of their estate delayed until after their spouse dies. However, they also wish to assure the designation of the ultimate beneficiaries of their assets. A common technique is to set up, through their will, a QTIP trust. This gives the spouse full income of the assets during their lifetime, while either designating the ultimate principal beneficiaries or limiting the surviving spouse to designate the beneficiaries from among the decedent's children or other delineated heirs.

Having the funds in the QTIP trust keeps the funds free from creditors' reach, creates a pool of ultimate beneficiaries the decedent chose, and permits all the income to be paid to the surviving spouse providing financial security similar to what they would have had they had the funds outright in their names.

CHAPTER 18

CHOOSING A GUARDIAN
FOR MINOR CHILDREN

Probably the single most important aspect of a will where there are minor children is the need to appoint a Guardian who will take care of the children in the event of the death of both parents. Following are some comments to help in the process of considering such a choice.

1. The first step is for each parent to prepare a list of possible Guardians with each selection rated by their degree of responsibility, accessibility, geographic location, lifestyle, moral tenets, opinions on child raising and personal compatibility with the children. Other factors to consider are the people's ages, whether they have children, and the ages of their children.

2. The parents should compare their lists to see if there are any they both chose. Additionally, they should discuss every person on either list. What occurs sometimes is that the discussion centers in on someone not on either list initially.

3. Meetings and discussions with the potential candidates are essential before the final selection can be made. Parents should learn about the potential candidate's willingness to become the children's Guardian, their projected short and long-range plans, and viewpoints on issues that are crucial to the parents.

4. Guardians should be selected after satisfying all concerns and after serious discussions between the children's parents. It would be wise to choose an alternate guardian or guardians should the primary guardian become unable to fulfill the assigned duties of caring for the children.

5. Meetings with the selected guardians should be held on a periodic basis and should include the children. These sessions will provide a forum to elaborate on the current needs and plans for the children. The meetings will also permit the potential guardians to voice changes in their own lifestyle that might have a dramatic impact on the children. This may cause a change of the guardian based solely on indirect or unsaid impressions imparted and conveyed during these sessions. It would also give the potential guardians and the children opportunities to become familiar with each other.

6. An instructional letter or memorandum should be prepared for the guardians if it becomes necessary for them to assume their duties. This letter or memorandum should be an updated list of important, helpful details in providing for the children's well being. The details should include the children's favorite foods, allergies, medical requirements, family medical history, personality traits and behavior responses. Personal opinions should also be stated on areas of personal discretion including spending allowances, dating, education, driving and drinking.

7. The will should specify which assets or the amount that should be placed in a trust with a trustee given the power to disburse them as required by the guardians for the care, maintenance, health, education and general well being of the children. This Trust will insure that essential assets needed to support the children can be used immediately without any court restrictions. This trust will expire at such time as pre-chosen by you in your will. An alternative to using the will would be a living trust (explained elsewhere).

8. The children's financial security and standard of living will be determined by the guardians, trustees and most importantly, by the parents' planning. The parents must provide direction as to the spending of funds to achieve their desired short-range and long-range goals. The guardians and trustees need to be provided with instructions of which goals have priority. For instance, are short-range goals such as a car or a vacation in Europe more important than long-range goals such as a college education or a nest egg for a future profession, business or house?

9. Day-to-day spending needs of the guardian can be provided for by establishing a monthly minimum allowance to pay the guardians. The parents should review the initial monthly amount periodically to see that it is still reasonable. Once the parents die, this amount will then be set. Afterwards, the trustee

can be provided with the power to increase the monthly allowance to meet predetermined specified spending goals or to simply adjust for inflation.

10. The monthly allowance will give the guardians the freedom to budget and plan their new responsibility without having to account to the trustee. In the event additional funds are required by the guardian requests can be made to the trustee. Further, at that time, a discussion with someone possibly knowledgeable or financially independent might be in order—the trustee.

11. The ability to maintain the monthly allowance is directly related to the liquid earning power of the remaining available assets. The parents should analyze the earning potential of the assets when drawing up their will in terms of after tax funds available for the guardian. An important consideration is that this earning power could sharply decline should the assets be substantially depleted to achieve a spending goal. Needless to say, much care should be used in projecting future cash flow as well as future budget requirements.

12. In addition to the monthly allowance, the will or trust could specify which items of care the trust should disburse without question by the trustee. This might include lessons, schooling, certain trips, religious instruction, and private tutoring.

13. If there are provisions for delayed distributions of the principal and interest to the children, the will or trust should state when distributions of income and principal is to be made as certain ages or stages are attained. See next chapter for more details on this.

14. You also have to designate the point when the monthly payments to the guardian would cease. I would suggest it stops one year after the youngest child graduates college, honorably discharged from the service or moves out of the guardian's house or age 24, whichever occurs first.

15. We do not advise making the guardians the trustees. A trustee should have no interest in the funds other than to see that your wishes and desires for your children can be attained and will be followed.

CHAPTER 19

HOW ASSETS CAN BE LEFT TO A MINOR

Under state laws, children cannot own financial assets until they reach majority—usually on their 18th birthday. Also, many times people do not want to leave assets outright to children or others until they attain a more mature age when they feel the children could better handle the funds. To delay the transfer of funds to a child, a trust needs to be established.

Following is an illustration of how funds could be left in a trust to a child or any other young beneficiary that will inherit funds.

- A separate trust should be established for each child. In lieu of separate trusts there possibly could be one trust that is "subdivided" into sub-trusts for each beneficiary.

- At age 21, the child will get distributions equivalent to the trust income. Upon reaching their 25th birthday, they will receive 1/3 of the total accumulated funds set aside for that child. The full income on the remaining funds will accumulate and be added to the undistributed principal. At age 30, half of the remaining funds will be distributed to that child. The income on the remaining funds will be added to principal with the full remaining amount distributed to the child at age 35.

- To the extent individual income taxes will have to be paid by a child on any income accumulated but not paid or distributed, there will be a distribution to cover the taxes. The amount distributed will be at the highest effective tax bracket the child is in for the year the income is taxed.

- The trustee will have the right to invade principal for ascertainable standards of health, education, and general well-being of the beneficiary.

- The trustee will have discretionary powers to make distributions for anything that the trustee believes will be in the child's best interest.

The above is an example of the available choices. It does not consider special needs of the child such as medical or custodial care or special schooling.

CHAPTER 20

PAYMENTS TO A GUARDIAN

Upon the death of both parents a guardian for minor children will be designated and appointed. Funds could be left to the children as described in the previous chapter. An additional provision could be included to provide funds to be used for the children's care by their guardian.

Following is an illustration of how this could be done.

- The designated legal guardian of the children would receive a net after tax income of $3,000 [or any chosen amount] per month until the youngest child reaches age 21 and they are not attending a four year college program; or if they are attending a four year college program or in the armed services, then until one year after they graduate, or are honorably discharged from the service, or the child reaches age 24, whichever occurs earlier. There will be no accountability of these funds.

- The trustee will have the right to make interest free loans or mortgages to the guardian, if in trustees opinion, the purpose of the loan is to assure or provide for the comfort (to be defined as loosely or liberally as possible) of the person in fulfilling their responsibilities as guardian of the children. The loans could have a maximum principal stated such as $400,000; and can have a maximum term such as ten or twenty years, or one year after the guardianship ends.

- The trustee will also have the right to withdraw principal or income at their discretion to apply for the benefit of the children or guardian if in the trustee's opinion such funds would benefit the children or the guardian's care of the children.

CHAPTER 21

A "GIFT" FOR YOUR CHILDREN

I do a lot of estate planning, primarily for wealthy older people, but the most satisfying planning is when my clients make a "gift" of a will, insurance trust and annual premiums of a life insurance policy to their children.

Few young people think about their demise, and fewer consider the husband and wife dying together, yet it is a possibility and needs to be considered and planned for should that terrible thing occur. This is a critical issue where there are young children.

Parents of young children are negligent if they do not plan for the possibility that they will die together prematurely. This planning requires they have a will with proper arrangements made for a guardian of their choosing with adequate funding available for the guardian to receive that eliminates the financial burden of caring for the children.

Will for Parents

Without a will, confusion will reign, unnecessary costs will build up, there will be delays in care for the children and possible conflicts of who will provide that care, uncertainty as to how much money would be available, who would manage it and make distribution decisions, and court appointed overseers of the guardians and others involved in their well being.

With a will, the parents provide the best shot for the proper care of their children. The will would designate a guardian, what funds they will receive, who will manage the money, and provisions for contingencies that will develop. Details are presented in the preceding chapters.

Life Insurance Policy

In addition to a will, the grandparents can purchase of a life insurance policy on their children's lives. A $1 million term policy with no extras or waivers for a fixed term of 20 or 30 years will cost a 30 year old about $75 per month. Premiums will vary based on health, age, policy term, and whether the policies will be split between the two parents.

$1 million invested reasonably conservative can provide a minimum of $30,000 income per year with part of that given to the guardian. If $1 million is not deemed sufficient, then 1) more insurance can be obtained, and 2) consider what would be available if there was no life insurance.

A note about life insurance coverage: There are many reasons to acquire or invest in a life insurance policy. That is not being covered, discussed or debated here. What I am suggesting is a policy to *secure the future cash flow* for the people that will be taking care of the children in the unlikely event of a premature death of both parents. The people buying this insurance should pray that they "waste" their money and never collect. However, this is insurance protection for a specific purpose for a specific period to serve a specific need. Afterwards that protection would not be needed. That is what I am talking about, and nothing else.

A second note about life insurance: It might be advisable for one or both of the parents to have life insurance to provide funds to the survivor in the event of one of them dying prematurely. This should also be considered. A way to handle this is to split the coverage between the two parents—with half (or any other proportion) coverage on each.

Irrevocable Life Insurance Trust

The life insurance should be purchased in an irrevocable life insurance trust ("ILIT"). The child being insured will be the grantor and one of their parents would be the trustee or any other trustee of their choosing. There might be a little bother—see instructions for an ILIT—with the formalities of the ILIT, but the benefits will be that, in the unlikely event of the there being proceeds, the insurance will remain outside of the direct control of anyone except the person the deceased appointed. Additionally the proceeds will be disbursed in accordance with the wishes of the grantor, and to whom and when and what to do if there is a greater need for funds than the annual income. Further, the funds in the trust cannot be attached or pass to anyone other than the beneficiaries named by the grantor. Finally, the funds in the trust, if properly administered, will never be subject to estate taxes.

CHAPTER 22

BOW WOW AND MEOW

Animal lovers that consider pets part of their family should make arrangements for them while they are able. Most people won't and cannot do what Leona Helmsley did, but you can make suitable and affordable provisions.

You can fund pet trusts using a living trust, or through your will. In either event, you will set aside some money to provide for their continued care in event of your death or disability.

Pet trusts are not much different from other types of trusts. The person establishing the trust appoints a trustee to manage the funds; and designates a caregiver who will receive the funds as needed from the trustee. When the last surviving pet dies, the remaining funds will be distributed as specified in the trust. Many states have per trust laws including New Jersey and New York, but they are different and, as with establishing all trusts, you must speak with a knowledgeable attorney before you decide how to proceed.

This is not much different from the process for choosing a guardian for minor children. Except in cases of very large funding in the trust, I suggest considering making the trustee and caregiver the same person.

An alternative is a pet retirement home or sanctuary. This is something you can find out about from your vet. In many cases, this will require more funding than with a pet trust and your choice of the residuary beneficiary of the remaining funds might be restricted to the sponsor of the sanctuary.

CHAPTER 23

IRA, 401K, 403B, ROTH IRA, ROTH 401K AND OTHER PENSION PLANNING

IRAs and pensions (including 401k and 403b accounts) generally comprise the largest portions of many non-business owners' estates after their residences. Yet, many people fail to plan adequately, or at all, for this most major asset.

Many people with IRAs and pensions limit their activities to filling out the designation of beneficiary forms their banks, brokers or insurance companies provide. The need for planning for IRAs and pensions is extremely critical. Following are just a few comments on how important planning is in this area. I suggest that you meet with your financial advisor to discuss how you want your IRAs and pension plans left to your heirs.

Note that IRAs and pensions distributions, except for Roth IRA or Roth 401k distributions, will be subject to income tax by the recipient.

Beneficiaries not determined by will

IRAs and pensions are included in the estate and are subject to estate taxes, but those accounts do not pass thorough the estate and the beneficiaries are not determined by the will. The beneficiaries are determined by designation of beneficiaries forms provided to plan trustees by the account owner.

Actually, IRA and pensions can pass through estates where the estate is named as a beneficiary, or is a default beneficiary—situations that represent bad tax planning in most situations. I do not recommend naming estates as beneficiaries unless it is the subject of careful planning with qualified advisors.

Advising beneficiaries what to do with an inherited IRA, 401k, 403b and pensions

Part of getting your affairs in order is to warn beneficiaries by leaving instructions that would be looked at before anything is done about certain assets they will be inheriting that could be troublesome if not handled properly. This includes inherited IRAs.

Beneficiaries should be advised to not do anything with an inherited IRA or pension before speaking to a *knowledgeable* tax advisor. They should not change the names on the account; and should not take, deposit or receive ANY distributions. Doing the wrong thing could make the entire IRA taxable in the year of the IRA owner's death instead of allowing the distributions to be taxed over the beneficiaries' life expectancies or the IRA owner's remaining life expectancy.

The account name should be kept in the name of the deceased IRA owner and have the beneficiary's name added as follows:

> **John Smith, deceased (date of death, January 4, 2012), for benefit of Susan Brown [designated beneficiary] (soc. sec. # 123-45-6789), beneficiary.**

When the name is changed to the beneficiary's name, the longest the distribution can be delayed would be until the end of the fifth year following the year of death.

If the name is *not* changed, the distributions for the beneficiaries could be made over the remaining life expectancy of the beneficiary if the death occurred before the required beginning date, or the distributions are based upon the withdrawal rate in effect during the owner's lifetime if death occurred after the required beginning date.

Irrespective of what is done, a spouse still has the right to roll over the funds into their own IRA. If the name is changed to surviving spouse's name it is deemed a spousal rollover.

Splitting Up Your IRA

You can divide your IRA into as many separate accounts as you so desire. Each account can have different beneficiaries or sets of beneficiaries. Also, your total annual minimum required distributions can come out of one or more accounts and does not have to come out of each separate account each year. Your choices can change from year to year.

Part of decluttering would be to combine IRA accounts, or move all your IRAs to one custodian. Obviously, if you have your IRAs spread over a number of banks to get higher or bonus interest this cannot be done, but combining them as much as possible simplifies things tremendously.

Contingent beneficiaries

You should name beneficiaries who will take the place of a deceased primary beneficiary. Post death planning to reduce income taxes or the estates of the subsequent IRA beneficiaries might be able to be done depending upon who the alternates are. This is something that needs to be discussed with a financial professional.

Proper planning can have the IRA become a legacy that will create wealth for generations of family members. For instance, an IRA inherited by an infant grandchild designated as beneficiary can provide distributions for over eighty or more years of their lifetime.

IRA rollovers

When you terminate your employment, you are given choices, and in some cases it is mandatory, to rollover your pension to an IRA. It can be done tax-free as long as the funds are rolled over from the plan directly to an IRA account, or if you take the funds directly and deposit in an IRA within sixty days. The best way is to have direct transfers made. You can open an IRA account with any bank, broker or insurance company without any deposit, get the account number and transfer instructions, and provide them to your employer.

If given the choice, it is generally better to rollover to an IRA than to leave with your former employer. IRAs give you much more flexibility in investment planning. Employer plans must provide for minimum distributions to spouses even in situations where there are prenuptial agreements or second marriages, while IRAs do not have these requirements. And employer plans have a 20% withholding tax requirement for distributions that IRAs do not have.

Keep copies of all forms you sign

Copies should be kept of all forms signed regarding your IRA plan. This includes a copy of the actual plan and any amendments; signed designation of beneficiary forms; withdrawal or distribution forms or requests; voluntary nondeductible contribution information; and correspondence between you and the trustee.

Many times the trustee changes because of a merger or acquisition of the trustee's bank, broker or insurance company. Papers get misplaced and lost. The burden of proof of what you decided remains on you, or your heirs, which makes it an even harder task. Signed and dated copies provide all the assurance you need.

Roth IRAs

If you converted an IRA to a Roth IRA you should retain the documentation. When there are eventual distributions under the proper circumstances, there will be no income tax on such withdrawals. Note that there might be estate tax and arrangements should be made to cover that tax on the Roth IRA accounts or the beneficiaries will be forced to withdraw money to pay that estate tax.

IRA Required Minimum Distribution Starting Date Table

	Sample	Sample	Fill in your #
Date of birth	June 1, 1942	Dec 1, 1942	
Date attained age 70	June 1, 2012	Dec 1, 2012	
Date attained age 70½	Dec 1, 2012	June 1, 2013	
Required beginning date	April 1, 2013	April 1, 2014	
Attained age during the calendar year age 70 ½ was attained (used for life expectancy purposes)	Age 70	Age 71	
Life expectancy to use	26.2	25.3	
IRA valuation date for first payment	Dec 31, 2011	Dec 31, 2012	
IRA valuation date for second payment	Dec 31, 2012	Dec 31, 2013	
Note: Where the life expectancy is based on a joint life, you use as the attained age of the designated beneficiary the age on their birthday that falls in the calendar year the IRA owner attained age 70½.			

Life expectancy tables

The tables on this and the following page can be used to estimate approximate life expectancy.

Joint "average" life expectancy table

This table provides approximate average joint life expectancies based on the age of the older person. This is the table used to determine IRA minimum required distributions.

Uniform distribution table
(based upon the age of the IRA owner on their
birthday in the year of the distribution)

(This table is not applicable where a spouse more than ten years younger is the designated beneficiary.)

Applicable Age	Divisor	Applicable Age	Divisor
70	27.4	93	9.6
71	26.5	94	9.1
72	25.6	95	8.6
73	24.7	96	8.1
74	23.8	97	7.6
75	22.9	98	7.1
76	22.0	99	6.7
77	21.2	100	6.3
78	20.3	101	5.9
79	19.5	102	5.5
80	18.7	103	5.2
81	17.9	104	4.9
82	17.1	105	4.5
83	16.3	106	4.2
84	15.5	107	3.9
85	14.8	108	3.7
86	14.1	109	3.4
87	13.4	110	3.1
88	12.7	111	2.9
89	12.0	112	2.6
90	11.4	113	2.4
91	10.8	114	2.1
92	10.2	115 and older	1.9

Single life expectancy table

Age	Life Expectancy	Age	Life Expectancy	Age	Life Expectancy
5	77.7	41	42.7	77	12.1
6	76.7	42	41.7	78	11.4
7	75.8	43	40.7	79	10.8
8	74.8	44	39.8	80	10.2
9	73.8	45	38.8	81	9.7
10	72.8	46	37.9	82	9.1
11	71.8	47	37.0	83	8.6
12	70.8	48	36.0	84	8.1
13	69.9	49	35.1	85	7.6
14	68.9	50	34.2	86	7.1
15	67.9	51	33.3	87	6.7
16	66.9	52	32.3	88	6.3
17	66.0	53	31.4	89	5.9
18	65.0	54	30.5	90	5.5
19	64.0	55	29.6	91	5.2
20	63.0	56	28.7	92	4.9
21	62.1	57	27.9	93	4.6
22	61.1	58	27.0	94	4.3
23	60.1	59	26.1	95	4.1
24	59.1	60	25.2	96	3.8
25	58.2	61	24.4	97	3.6
26	57.2	62	23.5	98	3.4
27	56.2	63	22.7	99	3.1
28	55.3	64	21.8	100	2.9
29	54.3	65	21.0	101	2.7
30	53.3	66	20.2	102	2.5
31	52.4	67	19.4	103	2.3
32	51.4	68	18.6	104	2.1
33	50.4	69	17.8	105	1.9
34	49.4	70	17.0	106	1.7
35	48.5	71	16.3	107	1.5
36	47.5	72	15.5	108	1.4
37	46.5	73	14.8	109	1.2
38	45.6	74	14.1	110	1.1
39	44.6	75	13.4	110+	1.0
40	43.6	76	12.7		

Sample Letter
When There are Multiple IRA Accounts and Minimum
Required Distribution Will Come Out of Another Account

Insert name and address of IRA Owner at top of letter

Account #_____

Date_____

Name of IRA Custodian_____
Address_____
City_____State_____Zip_____

Dear Sir or Madam:

Thank you for advising me of my required minimum distribution amount for the year
_____.

Please be advised that I have taken distributions from my other retirement accounts to satisfy the minimum distribution requirement.

Cordially,

_____

Sample Letter to IRA Beneficiaries

Insert name and address of IRA Owner at top of letter

Warning letter to seek professional assistance

Dear_____,

You have been named as a beneficiary of my IRA.

You should seek personal guidance BEFORE you request or accept any distribution from the account. You should not change the names on the account; and should not take, deposit or receive ANY distributions. Doing the wrong thing could make the entire IRA taxable in the year of my death instead of allowing the distributions to be taxed over either your life expectancy or my remaining life expectancy, depending on when I died. Also, receiving any distribution can ruin your chances to have tax planning done for you or your family such as making a qualified disclaimer.

I hope you make the most of this inheritance.

Good luck!

With love,

_____

CHAPTER 24

PENSION CHOICES

For many people, the pension plan their employer provides will comprise the greatest portion of their retirement income. Therefore, it is imperative that they understand the choices and how they relate to the income they, and possibly their spouse will depend on. Some of the rules and definitions are described below, but the best way to understand what you will receive is to meet with an HR person and/or an adviser provided by your employer.

Some definitions:

Annuity is any series of payments.

Annuitant is the person receiving annuity payments.

Lifetime annuity is a series of payments for the rest of someone's life.

Guaranteed period annuity is a series of payments that are guaranteed for a specific time.

Life expectancy is the age someone is expected to live based on previously determined data by insurance companies and the IRS. IRS tables are shown elsewhere in this book.

Joint life expectancy is the age at least one member of a couple is expected to live. This is usually a greater period than the single life expectancy for either of the two members. An example might be a man age 70 that has a life expectancy to age 88 who is married to a woman age 70 that has a life expectancy to age 91. On a joint basis, the life expectancy of at least one of the two of them is 94. Of course, actual life spans will vary from person to person.

Single life annuity is a series of payments for the rest of one person's life.

Two life annuity is a series of payments that stops on the death of the last person to die.

Factors affecting the amount of an annuity are:

- the amount of the accumulation when payments start,
- the age of the annuitant, or annuitants if two people, when the payments will start,
- whether the payments will be delayed or deferred,
- in cases where the accumulation continues to earn income, the amount or rate of earnings, and how the rate is determined and how often it will change, and
- in cases where there are annual expenses or fees, the amount or rate of reductions from the asset balance, or charges to annual payments.

Fixed annuity is where the pension or annuity payments do not change.

Cost of living increases are provided for in some plans. These are usually made once each year. You should also review the basis for the adjustments.

Two life annuity options are choices on how an annuity will be paid. Some plan choices are only available to spouses, and others permit non-spouse partners or others.

Full benefit to survivor is a pension where the payment does not change upon the death of the first person.

Half benefit to second person is where the person with the pension receives full payments during their life. When they die, the second person will receive half of what the first person received. If the second person dies first, there is no change even though only one partner remains. Payments stop at the death of the second to die. There can be any variation of percentages.

Two-thirds benefit to survivor is where the benefits drop to 2/3 of the pre death amount upon the death of either person. There can be any variation of percentages. The thing to be aware of is that the "cost" of any survivor benefits is a reduced annuity to the primary person receiving the pension.

Pension choice discussion and comments:

1. The highest payments go to a single life annuity that ends on the annuitant's death. Each item or feature that is added will decrease the payments.

2. The strategies employed will depend on whether there is a continuing need for the second person to receive the pension, and whether some amounts are left to other beneficiaries. For instance, a single life annuity with a ten-year guaranteed period will continue to be paid after the death of the annuitant until ten years of payments have been made (counting from the date of the first payment).

3. Two life annuities are the most common for couples. That assures income for the balance of either life. However, the percentage paid to the survivor varies greatly based upon individual circumstances and desires.

4. Adding a ten-year or twenty-year guarantee will further reduce the annual annuity payment. The guarantee amount usually assures that some payments will go to beneficiaries if there are early deaths of the annuitants. This provides for assets to be passed to beneficiaries at the expense of lower payments to the annuitants. Sometimes a fixed period low premium term insurance policy might be less costly to do.

5. Annuity recipients pay income taxes on the payments received. The income that is taxed is the amount received that is greater than the annuitant's investment or after tax contributions in the insurance contract or pension payment.

6. Spousal rights to pension income is provided by federal law. A spouse has the right to receive at least half of the retirement benefits. This can be waived, but waivers included in prenuptial agreements do not apply. The waiver must have been made after the marriage. This applies for annuities where the spouse is not the second annuitant for at least 50% of the benefits. People with same sex marriages need to check this with their employer or payer of the pension. *Note: the 50% spousal right does not apply to IRA accounts.*

7. If the annuitant dies before starting distributions or if a non lifetime annuity payout was selected, the total accumulation allocated to the annuitant becomes a death benefit payable to the beneficiary.

8. Also some plans allow the beneficiaries to withdraw the current or present value of the unpaid benefits in a lump sum, or to elect to receive them under a different payout schedule. Note that the current or present value is much less than the sum of the expected payments you would receive because the expected future earnings are not included in the payments. Additionally the discount is based on an earnings factor that might be greater than realistic market conditions at that time, making the present value even lower. If this is the situation, you should review your alternatives with a CPA, financial planner or consultant.

9. If the beneficiary is the surviving spouse, there are a number of choices that can be selected from:

   a. Lump sum payouts can be rolled over tax free into the surviving spouses own IRA account no later than the later of the December 31 of the fifth year following the year of the spouse's death, or the end of the year the deceased spouse would have attained age 70 ½.
   b. Periodic distributions can be selected starting by either the December 31 of the year following the year of death.
   c. Periodic distributions can be selected to start by the end of the year the deceased spouse would have attained age 70 ½, if later than "b".

10. If the beneficiary is not the surviving spouse the choices are limited and more restrictive and depends upon whether the lifetime annuity payments have already started.

    a. If the lifetime annuity payments have already started, the beneficiary has until the December 31 of the year following the year of death to select on income options.
    b. If an income option is not selected the entire accumulation must be withdrawn either in a single payment or periodic payments by the December 31 of the fifth year after death. Some plans have default options that might supersede this.
    c. If the lifetime annuity payments have not started, the choice has to be made by the December 31 of the year following the year of death. The decisions are whether to take a lump sum payment; a single life annuity with or without a guaranteed period, or a fixed period annuity less than the beneficiary's life expectancy or minimum required distribution payments, i.e. the smallest annual payout based on IRS rules.

11. Caution: the rules for non-spouse distributions are very complicated and exact. A non spouse beneficiary should not do anything and should not receive anything or sign anything without consulting with a professional financial advisor knowledgeable in these matters. Once something is done it becomes irrevocable and can greatly affect the amount of income taxes that will be paid on the pension amounts.

12. A strategy for a surviving spouse under age 59 ½ when their spouse dies and they intend to roll over most, but not all, of the pension accumulations is that they should withdraw what they want from the accumulation before it is rolled over into their IRA. Once they roll it over into the IRA, any withdrawals by them before they attain age 59 ½ would be subject to a 10% IRS penalty.

CHAPTER 25

SOCIAL SECURITY AND MEDICARE

Most people working in the United States will be eligible to collect Social Security retirement benefits and Medicare coverage when they attain the required ages.

Social Security coverage includes death, survivor and disability benefits, benefits to people who are blind, benefits to ex-spouses, and benefits to disabled minor children or where a disability started before age 22, or minor children if the parent is over age 65.

Medicare coverage starts at age 65 unless you are disabled and certain other circumstances.

Part of getting you affairs in order needs you to make sure your earnings have been entered properly. Unfortunately, the Social Security Administration has suspended issuing earnings record statements. If you have a prior issued statement you can review that. Otherwise, you should go on line to www.ssa.gov and go to **Estimate Your Retirement Benefits** and complete the requested information.

If you discover an error, or believe there is an error, contact a local Social Security office and discuss this with them. You can also contact the local office to ask to review your record.

If there is an error and it is not corrected, you may lose your opportunity to correct it and it could affect your benefits.

If you are over age 62 you should find out all you options for collecting Social Security. You can start collect anytime after then. I recommend a visit to a local Social Security office to discuss this with them. They are extremely helpful and will explain all your options.

CHAPTER 26

INCAPACITY

Part of getting your affairs in order is to consider the possibility of becoming incapacitated. Obviously, this is an important issue. Following are some points to consider in this regard:

1. The incapacity can be either mental or physical, and can continue until recovery or death. Any arrangements made can be revoked or changed anytime if the person is in control of their faculties.

2. In the absence of proper arrangements, if someone becomes unable to care for them self or their affairs, it might be necessary for their family to resort to the courts for direction, and the appointment of a Conservator or Guardian. This might turn out to be a cumbersome and unpleasant experience that would not be to their best interest.

3. An alternative plan can be set up whereby someone is authorized to act for them and handle their affairs pursuant to a Durable Power of Attorney (explained in a separate chapter) executed while they are in good health.

4. Instead of, or in addition to the Power of Attorney, a Revocable Living Trust can be used. The trust can have a limited amount of cash or liquid assets in it with the trustee set up to immediately act if there is an incapacity. Multiple living trusts can be established. This one would be for the single purpose of making cash available if needed during a period of incapacity.

5. A standby trust can also be used as a receptacle for the assets transferred by the Attorney-In-Fact to Trustees who might have broader or more specific powers.

A standby trust is a revocable trust created to handle or manage a person's assets while they are incapacitated or otherwise cannot manage their affairs (they could be out of the country for an extended period or have an operation with a long rehabilitation period).

6. You can also open a new bank account, and give a limited durable power so there would be available funds that could be used in the event of incapacity.

7. Alternatively, a joint bank account can be opened with a limited or a fixed amount of available funds that can be accessed by the co-owner if there is incapacity and the cash is needed.

CHAPTER 27

POWER OF ATTORNEY

Powers of attorney give another person the rights to act on their behalf. This is done so that a person's affairs can be handled, continued or dealt with should they become incapacitated. There are different types of powers of attorney and great care should be taken when giving someone that power.

Powers are only valid if the person executing the power is in full control of their faculties. Incompetent people cannot grant these powers. Where there is no power of attorney appointed, and if it is necessary for someone else to take over the affairs of an incompetent person, they must go to court to become appointed.

Powers of attorney can be limited or general or however else the power specifies. A limited power is restricted to a specific or special activity such as the control over a specific bank or brokerage account, or the power to represent a taxpayer before a tax authority but to not receive any funds. A general power is broad and can cover everything the person granting the power can do. The person with the power is called the "attorney-in-fact" and can have or assume complete control over the grantor's assets.

Powers of attorney become void if the person granting the power becomes incapacitated (either physically or mentally) unless the grantor specifies that the power will continue after incapacity. That is called a durable power. All powers end at the grantor's death.

Provisions in powers of attorney allowing the designated agent to make gifts should be specified or denied. While this could reduce estate tax rather significantly in some situations, it could also have gifts made of all of a person's assets against their wishes. So caution should be used when granting the power to make gifts.

Edward Mendlowitz, CPA

Separate states may have special rules for the designations of an Attorney-In-Fact under a Durable Power. This should be checked with a local attorney.

Health Care Power of Attorney is a form that allows the designation of an agent or someone besides you to make health care decisions. This is limited to health care decisions and not to anything else. See separate section.

CHAPTER 28

LIVING WILL AND HEALTH CARE PROXY

It is has become a standard procedure for many people to establish a "Living Will" or a "Health Care Proxy" which are documents that set forth desires should they become incapacitated or incurably ill. Some states recognize the validity of these wills and documents while others will accept it as a guide to the wishes but not necessarily binding upon the court.

This is an area that should more appropriately be discussed with a local attorney. Following is some information that can serve as a guide to deciding what to do in this regard.

The terms health care proxy and health care power of attorney are used interchangeably. A living will generally is more limited or less broad in scope than a health care proxy and can refer to a point in time. Depending upon the state, your attorney's instructions and the policy of the health care provider, one form over the other might be preferable. This is extremely important, and you are advised to discuss this with an attorney.

Except to the extent stated otherwise, these documents give the person named as the agent the authority to make any and all health care decisions for the signor if they are not capable of making them their self. The agent's authority begins when the treating doctor certifies that there is a lack of capacity to make health care decisions. The person acting on their behalf should make any decisions in accordance with previously stated wishes to them. Religious and moral beliefs should also have previously been explained. The agent should become familiar with all their obligations and responsibilities.

Because "health care" means any treatment, service or procedure to maintain or diagnose, and can be for a physical or mental condition, the agent has the power to make a broad range of health care decisions. The agent may consent, refuse to consent, or withdraw consent to medical treatment and may make decisions about withdrawing or withholding life supporting treatment. There are certain things that the agent may not be permitted to consent to (such as voluntary inpatient mental health services, convulsive treatment, psychosurgery, or abortion) and this should be specifically discussed with an attorney. A physician must comply with the agent's instructions or allow the patient to be transferred to another physician.

It is important that the signor discuss what they want with their physician or other health care provider before the health care proxy is signed to make sure that the nature and range of decisions that may be made on behalf of the signor is fully understood. If the signor does not have a physician, they should talk with someone else who is knowledgeable about these issues and can answer the questions. Anyone granting such powers should make sure they fully understand the document before it is signed.

The person appointed as agent should be someone known and trusted and should be at least 18 years of age.

If someone is appointed as a health or residential care provider (e.g., your physician or an employee of a home health agency, hospital, nursing home, or residential care home, other than a relative), that person has to choose between acting as an agent or as the health or residential care provider. The law does not permit a person to do both at the same time.

The person appointed should be informed that they are to be the health care agent. The agent and physician should be provided with a signed copy of the agreement. The people who have signed copies should be indicated on the document itself. The agent is not liable for health care decisions made in good faith on behalf of the signor.

Even after there are signed documents, the signor retains the right to make health care decisions for them self as long as they are able to do so. Treatment cannot be given or stopped over the signor's objection. The signor has the right to revoke the authority granted to the agent by informing the agent, health or residential care provider orally or in writing, or by execution of a subsequent durable power of attorney for health care.

Alternates can be designated in the event the agent is unwilling, unable or ineligible to act. Any alternate agent that is designated has the same authority to make health care decisions as the primary agent.

CHAPTER 29

DISABILITY INCOME INSURANCE

Part of arranging your affairs is to provide for income if you become disabled. Not having adequate cash flow can affect your financial well being and security. It could also cause an erosion of your assets.

Disability income insurance provides a fixed income during periods of disability either through accident or sickness. Policies can be obtained personally, although most employers provide statutory disability insurance and some provide additional amounts as a fringe benefit. Check with your employer as to what coverage you have. You can also check to see if you can purchase additional coverage from the employer's insurance agent. Social Security also offers disability coverage. That, too, should be reviewed by you.

Definitions of disability, waiting periods, payment terms, lengths of payments and differences in coverage for accident or sickness vary with each insurance company so coverage should be reviewed and examined closely. Many disability income policies do not cover those past age 65. Make sure of what you have covered.

Chapter 30

Long Term Care Insurance

This insurance provides benefits in the event you cannot care for yourself under normal circumstances and covers care not usually covered by other types of insurance

Benefits are provided based on the insured's inability to perform the basic activities of daily living such as eating, toileting, dressing, getting in or out of bed and normal mobility. Benefits can be paid for in-house or facility care, and for part-time or full-time care.

Premiums are determined based on the age when the insurance is applied for, amount of coverage, whether there are inflation increases in benefits, your health when you apply, benefit period, waiting period until benefits start, and what defined circumstances will trigger benefits.

Policies are privately obtained and provide much wider coverage than Medicaid. Also benefit payments are not based on income and asset limitations. Certain premiums may also be deducted as health care insurance.

CHAPTER 31

OTHER INSURANCE COVERAGE

Following are brief descriptions of insurance coverage not usually obtained, or that is obtained in inadequate amounts. Part of getting affairs in order is to provide for your asset protection and having the proper coverage is part of this. Insufficient insurance can expose you to serious losses that could jeopardize your future financial comfort and security. Note that this chapter does not cover all types of insurance coverage that is needed and should not be used instead of normal sound judgment.

Umbrella insurance

We all have personal liability exposure. The financial impact and mental stress arising from a personal incident such as a terrible auto accident, an accident at home, a discrimination, personal libel or slander law suit or a large accident on your rental property can be devastating. This protection can be provided for at relatively low cost.

Excess personal liability or umbrella policies typically cover losses over the amount of your regular insurance coverage, or over stated minimum amounts of regular insurance coverage. Note that you are not covered for any gaps between the two.

Premiums can range from $300 for $1 million of coverage to about $1,000 for $5 million of coverage. Check your policy to what your coverage is, and the limits, and then call your broker to institute excess coverage.

Workers' Compensation

Workers' Compensation covers people that get hurt while they are working in your home.

This coverage extends to people even if they are not employed directly by you and possibly people working "off the books." An example is when you engage someone with a one-person business that installs dishwashers and he brings along a college kid as a helper, who he pays "off the books." The dishwasher falls and crushes the student's hand. Without the workers' comp insurance, you can be sued since the injury occurred in your home. With the workers' comp insurance, the injured person deals directly with the insurance carrier—you are out of the picture.

Each policy has defined coverage and exclusions. These must be carefully read and understood so that you are clear on your coverage.

I recommend getting a workers' compensation rider to your homeowner's policy as a safety precaution to protect your assets.

Unlicensed and Uninsured Contractors Insurance

In additional to workers' compensation coverage you should consider insurance for damages caused by unlicensed or uninsured contractors. Many policies routinely exclude damages done by such people. This includes noncompliance with building codes, lack of obtaining of permits, poor quality work that causes other damages, scams and broken contracts. Insurance for some of these are not normally available and you should be aware of what type of contractors or handy people you should not use.

Uninsured motorist

Most people have coverage to provide payments if they are in an accident caused by an uninsured motorist. However, in many cases they could be underinsured with coverage near the minimum range, rather than at the higher limits of coverage. This is relatively low cost insurance and you should consider amounts near the higher levels.

Further, many umbrella policies provide coverage for uninsured motorist damages with a $250,000 or $300,000 deductible. You need to make sure you have coverage for the full amount of the deductible, or there will be a gap that could be a cost to you should such a disaster occur.

Consult your insurance agent

You should make it a practice to meet at least once every two years with your insurance broker or agent to review your coverage, the cost, additional areas or coverage, available alternatives and ways to reduce premiums. Additionally, you should discuss with them the items mentioned above and elsewhere in this book as to their applicability to you.

Another word for coverage is protection. Make sure you are properly protected.

CHAPTER 32

BUSINESS AGREEMENTS

If you are an owner in a privately held business you need a buy-sell agreement. Such an agreement is similar to a will, but it is for the business. It is not right to neglect to have a will, and not having suitable arrangements for your business is equally negligent.

Further, having an agreement not only protects your family for the value of your business interests, but also protects the surviving partner because the transfer of their disabled or deceased partner's ownership will be easier in that a method, formula or price has been established. This reduces or eliminates any unpleasant negotiating with the deceased or disabled partner's family.

These agreements have various names depending upon the nature of the entity, and can be called shareholders' agreements, buy-sell agreements, members' agreement or partnership agreements. Whatever their name, they serve the same purpose—to say what happens to your ownership shares or interests upon your disability or death.

If you have an agreement, good for you, but try to review it at least once every two years for current applicability and values.

If you do not have one, make that one of your priorities. You owe it to yourself, your family and your partners.

CHAPTER 33

ESCHEAT

Unclaimed funds are turned over to the state who holds it as "custodian" for the rightful owners. These are done pursuant to state escheat laws.

Whether or not you believe you have unclaimed funds, it is a good policy to file a claim at least once every five years with each state you have lived in, or owned property in, or had a mailing address. You can go on-line to find your state's forms and make the claims. There are also services that will make the claims for you for a fee.

Many banks and brokers typically turn over accounts that are inactive every few years, and usually without notification. This can apply to long-term bank certificates of deposit, money market accounts and companies where there was a merger or reorganization and you have the actual stock certificates of the acquired company. One way to protect yourself is to monitor these accounts and send a letter of notification of activity to the institution with the account. See sample on next page.

Edward Mendlowitz, CPA

Sample Letter of Notification of Activity

Insert your name and address at top of letter

Account #_____

Date_____

Name of Institution or Company_____
Address_____
City_____State_____Zip_____

Dear Sir or Madam:

Please accept this letter as notification of activity for the above listed account.

This account should be considered as active and should remain with you as an active account.

If any questions, don't hesitate to contact me.

Cordially,

_____

CHAPTER 34

WHAT RECORDS YOU SHOULD KEEP

It is important to know what tax records you should keep and how long you should keep them. When organizing your files, please remember these are general rules concerning your records:

Income Tax Returns and Related Items

Keep all federal and state income tax returns and supporting documents (i.e., those items confirming your income and/or deductions) for a minimum of six years after the return's filing date. Why? The IRS can assess additional taxes within three years of its filing date, but has up to six years in which to make a tax assessment if the IRS determines that a substantial amount of income was omitted from the return.

Also, the tax returns and back up income data are a "road map" to facilitate settling your affairs or to assist someone handling your affairs. This will provide a very good idea of what assets you have and where they are. One method to follow is to put each year's return and data in an envelope marked with the year on it, and the date (six years later) you should dispose of it.

Gift Tax Returns

If you ever made gifts where you filed federal gift tax returns, those returns should be retained forever. Also, keep all back up with the returns. These returns might be needed to be filed with estate tax returns.

Mailing Receipts

If you mail your return by certified mail, or by an express carrier, keep the receipt with your copy of the tax return. Make sure the receipt shows the date the return was mailed. If your return is filed electronically, keep a copy of the electronic filing confirmation with a printed or CD backup copy of the return. In the event the return is misplaced or lost by the tax authority this documentation will save you from late filing or payment penalties.

Residential Property Records

The tax laws allow a tax-free amount when you sell your residence. However, you still might have to substantiate the amount of the gain. Because of this you need to keep closing statements from all home purchases and sales. In addition, keep records of the amounts that you spent for home improvements with this file.

Stock and Bond Records

Keep records of your investment (e.g., stock, mutual funds, and bonds) purchases. Besides providing you with a date for determining the type of gain—long-term versus short-term—these records establish your basis in the investment and help to compute the gain/loss when you sell them. In addition, keep records that show a return of capital dividends on your investments, and complete back up of DRIP (dividend reinvestment plans) additions which will establish your basis in those shares.

Tax tip: If you've owned DRIP stock for many years and do not have the back up information and want to dispose of those stocks, consider using them instead of cash to make your charitable contribution. You don't need your basis; you will get a deduction for the full value of the stock; and do not have to recognize the capital gain on those shares.

Keep all records showing your basis of inherited assets, or assets received by a gift. These will be needed if you sell the assets, and might be needed if you are involved in a marital separation.

Rental Real Estate Records

For any rental real estate or depreciable business property that you own, keep records of the property's cost, the purchase date, the method used to calculate depreciation, and a schedule of all depreciation claimed on the property in previous years. Maintain these records until you sell or dispose of the property. Once you sell the property, keep these records with the tax return on which you report the sale. You need to keep current leases handy, and I would also retain the immediate preceding lease for that property in case weird claims are made against you and you would need to refer to the lease.

Partnership and Business Agreements

You should retain all partnership, member, and/or corporate organizational, buy/sell or cross purchase agreements as long as you have an interest in any currently owned business interest or entity. You should also retain all basis calculations.

Employment Contracts

Any employment contracts, stock purchase, option, restricted stock or similar agreements should be retained as long as you are employed by the company and then at least through the date of expiration of any of the commitments should they go past your employment. It is important to have these handy if you die and there are limited exercise periods that survive you.

Personal Records

Keep a permanent file of personal records—such as marriage license, divorce agreements, prenuptial agreements, change of name papers, military discharge, family tree, birth certificates, and receipts for purchases of art, collectibles, jewelry and the like since they can provide a basis for determining your tax liability when you dispose of the property.

Other Records

There are other situations where you will benefit by keeping records. For example, if you have made nondeductible contributions to an IRA, maintaining records of these contributions will facilitate proving, and reducing, your tax liability when funds are withdrawn from the IRA. You should also retain Roth IRA conversions that were taxed. For this you can keep the tax return for the years the tax was paid.

Legal Judgments and Loan Satisfactions

I recommend keeping these forever. This is irrefutable proof that you do not owe those debts or obligations.

Insurance Policies

This listing refers to old documents. All current information should be kept in an easy to access place. This includes every type of insurance policy, and I would retain a minimum of two years' policies so that you would have a comparison if you need to make a claim, and to check rates and coverage.

In closing, the general rule is: When in doubt about a document, keep it.

CHAPTER 35

FUNERAL ARRANGEMENTS

Someone will be making your final arrangements. It should be you.

Only you are clear whether you want to be buried, cremated, placed in a crypt or whatever else can be done. You should also provide instructions for type of coffin or urn as well as wake, shiva, celebration, or party; and what will be in your obituary notice and where it should be published. Choices of clergy, funeral home, cemetery, stone or marker also need to be done.

Some arrangements can be prepaid, while others will be negotiated after your demise.

You may not care—so don't bother yourself with these details.

CHAPTER 36

LETTER OF INSTRUCTION TO FAMILY

Although not a formal part of an estate plan, many people choose to prepare a letter of instructions giving pertinent information they feel their family will need, or that will be helpful in the settling of their affairs.

Included with such a letter should be some of the data forms in here that you fill out.

This letter tells what items need to be addressed immediately such as funeral, burial or cremation instructions and people to notify.

A separate letter can also list preferred distributions of selected possessions such as sentimental items, jewelry, art or stamp or coin collections and similar articles.

Chapter 37

Ethical Will or Statement of Values

An ethical will or statement of values contain concerns that you want your children, grandchildren, or other heirs to know, learn from or be aware or. If you prepare such a statement, you should leave it in a place that would be looked at as soon as practical after your death.

Besides written documents, some people video or audio record themselves and their requests and charges.

Two people come to mind when I think of letters explaining personal values and "where I came from" or "how I got here" adventures—Benjamin Franklin and Randy Pausch. We all know who Benjamin Franklin is—just look on the $100 bill, or the back of the $2 bill (he is shown there signing the Declaration of Independence). Franklin wrote his autobiography in a series of letters to his son and then grandson to explain his beginnings and how his values developed throughout his formative years until he was in his 50s—he lived to be 84. He did not cover his public activities that they either knew about or would otherwise find out. The letters were made public after his death by being published as his autobiography by his grandson. The letters were intended for his family to influence them to follow good practices. Randy Pausch, a college professor, wrote *The Last Lecture* after he found out he was dying and wanted to document his thoughts for his young children. Both books are excellent and highly recommended.

You can do something similar. Buy a notebook and start writing. Spelling and grammar shouldn't be a concern. Put down your thoughts in any order you want. Once you start writing, the ideas, memories and points you want to make will flow off your pen (or computer keyboard, if you wish). The more the merrier and rambling is permitted and probably preferred since your personality will show through and be reflected to the reader.

Other examples of ethical wills or advice could be found in the Bible. Isaac and Jacob each gave final blessings to their children about their future activities. Moses gives a final exhortation to the Israelites just before he dies, when they are ready to enter the Land of Israel. Jesus words in John (14:15-17); Polonius' famous speech to Laertes in Shakespeare's *Hamlet*; and the final page of *The Good Earth* by Pearl Buck where Wang Lung tries to tell his sons the importance of keeping the land, are all excellent illustrations of a father's concern for his children's future.

Following is a brief listing of some of the things you can relate to your descendants.

- Your best accomplishments
- What you would have liked your best accomplishment to have been
- Your regrets
- Experiences you have learned from that your children wouldn't have known about
- What you would have done better that would have made your life better
- Experiences and/or people that have molded you or had a strong impact on you
- What you want for your children
- Things you value
- Things you believe in
- Religious feelings
- How you felt when you first found out you were going to die (or had cancer, or needed heart surgery) or when you woke from an emergency operation or a terrible accident
- What you would like said in your eulogy
- Favorite quotes
- Some books that might express your feelings

An excellent book on the topic is *Ethical Wills, 2nd Edition: Putting Your Values on Paper* by Barry K. Baines, M.D. This book contains a chapter on Living Wills and an appendix with extensive samples of Ethical Wills and Values' Statements. Another recommended book is *Tuesdays with Morrie: An Old Man, A Young Man, and Life's Greatest Lesson* by Mitch Albom.

A recommended novel by a bestselling author that gives examples of final letters and circumstances that caused their writing is *One Summer* by David Baldacci.

Hank Greenberg, the baseball great left an eloquent love letter to his wife telling her not to grieve because he had lived "a wonderful life" and part of it was his good fortune to have shared 25 years with her. He also said he thought he had done what he was supposed to do with his life.[4] What a nice final letter!

There are services that create a record of a person's life and preserve it on a DVD, CD or bound volume. To get an idea of what can be done go to www.lifestoriesremembered. net.

---

[4]   *Hank Greenberg: The hero who didn't want to be one* by Mark Kurlansky.

CHAPTER 38

CONCLUSION

Decluttering, getting your affairs in order, planning an estate and family asset transfer affairs are extremely important and should be done with much care.

The purpose of the planning is to try to leave your affairs in a reasonable manner during a difficult period for your loved ones. Preparing early will make it easier for those involved in settling your estate to fulfill your wishes and permit relative harmony among those receiving distributions.

However, keep in mind that even if the current process is completed with everything done in a "perfect" manner, this hopefully will not be the last effort in this regard. As circumstances change, there will be the opportunity to change, revise, amend and update what has been started and what has ended up being done. If this process is looked at as a beginning stage in what will be a life-long "work in process" I feel it will be easier to proceed.

WORKSHEETS

A digital file with all the worksheets will be emailed to you
if you request it by emailing me at emendlowitz@withum.com

Worksheet 1

Important Papers Listing and Checklist

Security is a warm calm feeling. There are many ways of protecting yourself. One way is making sure your affairs are in order.

Getting your affairs in order could be as simple as preparing a listing of where you keep your important papers. Other ways would be to make sure you have an updated will, health care proxy and living will. Following is a checklist where you could enter where you keep your important papers, and at the same time it could be used as a checklist of some things that you should have.

If info is indicated on tax return information such as annual 1099s or K-1s, state this.

Prepared by:_____ Date prepared:_____	Comments	Location
Your Will		
Spouse's Will		
Addendums, codicils or changes to will		
Powers of Attorney		
Living Will and Health Care Proxy		
Funeral Arrangements		
Birth Certificates		
Marriage License		
Divorce Papers		
Passports		

Other Personal legal papers such as change of name		
Military Discharge		
Family Tree		
Blood Bank location (if blood is needed by me)		
Other personal info (e.g. blood type, medical history)		
Real Estate Closing Contracts		
Mortgages Payable		
Notes Payable		
Deeds & Title Insurance		
Automobile Title(s)		
Judgments and satisfactions		
Loan, Mortgage, Levies and Lien Satisfactions		
Jewelry, art and collectibles bills of sale		
Jewelry, art and collectibles location		
Appraisals of any property		
Safe Deposit Box Location		
Stock Certificates		
Bonds		
Stock Options		
Stock Purchase Agreements		
Checking Account Documents or info		
Money Market Accounts info		
Savings Passbooks		
Certificates of Deposit		
Brokerage Account Info		
Notes Receivable		
Life Insurance Policies		
Disability Insurance Policies		
Medical Insurance Policies and Coverage Information		
Insurance Policies—Other		
Partnership and/or Corporate Agreements		
Employment Contracts		

Retirement Agreements		
IRA documents including designation of beneficiary forms		
Pension Plan Documents		
Profit Sharing Plan Documents		
Deferred Compensation Agreements		
Military benefits		
Income Tax Returns		
Gift Tax Returns		
Trust and Other Tax Returns (state type of return)		
Trust Documents		
Financial and Estate Plans Prepared by Self or Others		
Pending Contracts		
Passwords for Computers, Email and All other Accounts Requiring Passwords		
Other Records		
People to Call		
Accountant		
Attorney		
Banker		
Broker or financial planner		
Insurance Agent		
People to consider selling my art, jewelry or collectibles to		
Person or People with Access to my Personal Information		
Location of Letter of Instruction to Executor or Heirs or distribution list of jewelry and other precious or sentimental items		

WORKSHEET 2

CHECKLIST OF ESTATE PLANNING THINGS TO DO

This is a sampling of things that should be done. This checklist is preliminary to meeting with an attorney and some of the items might need explanations from your attorney. This checklist is not a substitute for legal advice that can only be provided by an attorney.

#	Description	Done (✓)	Comments
1	Make a listing of all assets and liabilities		
2	Prepare a listing of intended beneficiaries and secondary and successive beneficiaries		
3	Make a list of what distributions you would want to make to each beneficiary, including specific property		
4	Prepare a schedule of how your assets PLUS life insurance benefits and other assets not necessarily under your control, will be distributed to your heirs and beneficiaries. Determine if this meets with your wishes		
5	Decide if bequests will be made outright or in trust. If in trust, determine the terms of the disposition of the income and principal		
6	Decide who will be your executor and alternates. Decide if a bank will be ultimate alternate executor		
7	Decide who will be the trustees and alternates. Decide if a Bank will be ultimate alternate trustee		
8	Decide if statutory fees will be paid to executors and trustees		

9	Decide whether executors and trustees will need to obtain a bond		
10	Obtain copies of previously signed designation of beneficiary forms from every account needing one. Some accounts would be: IRA accounts, Roth IRA, 401k, 403b, Pension plans, Life insurance policies, and any other account maintained where a beneficiary may have been designated		
11	Meet with attorney		
12	Need a will		
13	Discuss with attorney if you should set up and transfer assets to a Living Trust.		
13a	If a Living Trust is set up, determine what assets will be transferred to it, and how and when, and who the ultimate trustee will be		
14	Health Care Proxy and Living Will. Determine need and who will be designated		
15	Durable Power of Attorney. Determine need and who will be designated and what powers they will have		
16	Determine need for a Limited Power of Attorney for a bank account with a limited amount of funds (say, $25,000 or any other amount considered necessary or appropriate).		
17	Decide if any bequests will be made to charitable organizations Decide if a charity will be an ultimate beneficiary if there are no other beneficiaries		
18	If a business is owned with others, there should be a shareholders, partnership, members buy/sell agreement-that has previously been executed. It should be reviewed to determine if it is still applicable, relevant or current If not owned with others, make arrangements for its sale or continuation after death of the owner		
19	Prepare a statement of values—religious, ethical, moral or social		
20	Listing of specific bequests of jewelry, art or items of sentimental value		

WORKSHEET 3

ESTIMATED ASSETS
TO BE INCLUDED IN ESTATE AND
POTENTIAL DISTRIBUTION TO BENEFICIARIES

This should be filled out based upon your existing will. If you have no will, then base the list on how you want to make your bequests. Use estimated amounts. Do not get caught up with exact details—use big picture amounts. The amounts will be different when you die. You may want to add categories or expand on what is shown below—the format is illustrated to get you started.

Item	Amount of asset to be included in estate	Distribution of estate assets							Items passing outside of estate but subject to estate taxes	
		Used to pay debts	Used to pay taxes	To trusts for child-ren	To QTIP trust for spouse	To spouse outright	To specific indivi-duals	To charities	Amount	Beneficiary

WORKSHEET 4

DESIGNATION SHEET

A separate sheet should be completed for each spouse or partner. This will be needed when you meet with an attorney to have will prepared.

Title	Designee	Relationship
Executor of Will		
Co-executor (if any)		
Alternate		
2nd Alternate		
QTIP Trust Trustee		
Co-Trustee (if any)		
Alternate		
2nd Alternate		
Credit Shelter Trust Trustee		
Co-Trustee (if any)		
Alternate		
2nd Alternate		
Life Insurance Trust Trustee		
Co-trustee (if any)		
Alternate		

2nd Alternate		
Living Trust Trustee		
Co-trustee (if any)		
Alternate		
2nd Alternate		
Guardian (a guardian is one person, not a couple)		
Alternate		
2nd Alternate		
Children's Trust Trustee		
Co-trustee (if any)		
Alternate		
2nd Alternate		

WORKSHEET 5

TERMS OF TRUSTS

Following is an outline to list terms of certain trusts. You can follow this to add other trusts.

Children's trust
Payments equal to earnings when child reaches age 21.   1/3 of principal upon reaching age 25, 1/2 of the remaining balance upon attaining age 30, the balance at age 35.   Alternatively, the trust can provide that a portion be distributed upon marriage, or receiving certain college or university degrees, honorable discharge from the armed forces, or the attainment of any other significant event in their lives.
To the extent individual income taxes will have to be paid by a child on any income accumulated but not paid or distributed, there will be a distribution to cover the taxes. The amount distributed will be at the highest effective tax bracket the child is in for the year the income is taxed.   The trustee will have the right to invade principal for ascertainable standards of health, education, and general well-being of the beneficiary.   The trustee will have discretionary powers to make distributions for anything that the trustee believes will be in the child's best interest.
Payments to Guardian from Children's Trust
The designated legal guardian of the children would receive a net after tax income of $3,000 [or any chosen amount] per month until the youngest child reaches age 21 and is not attending a four year college program; or if attending a four year college program or in the armed services, then until one year after graduation, or are honorably discharged from the service, or the child reaches age 24, whichever occurs earlier. There will be no accountability of these funds.

The trustee will have the right to make interest-free loans or mortgages to the guardian, if in trustees opinion, the purpose of the loan is to assure or provide for the comfort (to be defined as loosely or liberally as possible) of the person in fulfilling their responsibilities as guardian of the children. The loans could have a maximum principal stated such as $400,000; and can have a maximum term such as ten or twenty years, or one year after the guardianship ends.

The trustee will also have the right to withdraw principal or income at their discretion to apply for the benefit of the children or guardian if in the trustee's opinion such funds would benefit the children or the guardian's care of the children.

QTIP Trust

Payments of income quarterly for the rest of my spouse's life

Principal equally, per stirpes, to my children when my spouse dies

Credit Shelter Trust

Income to be distributed annually to any of the following at discretion of trustee: My spouse, children, and grandchildren, all per stirpes

Principal equally, per stirpes, to my children when spouse dies

Or

Income to be distributed annually to my spouse for rest of life

Principal equally, per stirpes, to my children when spouse dies

WORKSHEET 6

FACT SHEET

List the people you want to include in your will or trusts.

Name	Address	Relationship	Date of Birth

WORKSHEET 7

SPECIFIC BEQUESTS

Use this sheet to list specific items or amounts you want to leave to certain people.

Beneficiary	Item	Amount or estimated value

Worksheet 8

Balance Sheet

List your assets and liabilities. Approximate amounts are sufficient since the amounts will continuously change. The purpose of the balance sheet is to give you a place to list everything you own, and owe.

Prepared for:

Date prepared:

Asset	Account # (if applicable)	Amount or Value	Comment or who to contact
Cash accounts			
Brokerage accounts			
Retirement accounts			
Annuities			
Real Estate			

Residence			
Business			
Personal property			
Household furnishings			
Jewelry			
Art			
Collectibles			
Life insurance cash value			Death benefit:
Other assets			
Total assets		$	

Liabilities			
Credit cards			
Loans			
Mortgages (list property)			
Loan guarantees			
Loans co-signed			
Total liabilities			
Net worth			

Worksheet 9

Cash Flow and Income

List any income and cash flow that would not be obvious from reviewing tax returns. Include pension and annuity income, and cash flow from reverse mortgages, if any.

Include trusts you are a beneficiary of.

Item	Account #	Amount	Comment

WORKSHEET 10

LIFE INSURANCE

List all life insurance that covers you. Include policies you own, owned by others and trusts, coverage on loans and mortgages and employer provided policies.

Insurance Company or Employer	Policy #	Death Benefit	Annual premium	Due Date	Owned by	Beneficiary

WORKSHEET 11

PENSIONS AND ANNUITIES

List all pensions and annuities that cover you or that you will receive some day, or are receiving presently. Include annuity policies you own or owned by others and trusts.

Insurance Company or Employer	Policy #	Annual payment	Start date	End Date	Owned by	Beneficiary and payment terms to beneficiary

WORKSHEET 12

FINANCIAL OBLIGATIONS

List any financial debts and obligations such as loans that you guaranteed or co-signed, alimony or prenuptial agreements, commitments or contingencies from businesses, buy out commitments for a business, charitable obligations and pledges, and any other promises made that could create a liability or financial obligation.

_____
_____
_____
_____
_____
_____
_____
_____
_____
_____
_____
_____
_____
_____
_____
_____
_____
_____
_____
_____
_____
_____
_____
_____
_____
_____
_____

Worksheet 13

Checklist of Things to Get Rid of

This is a suggested list of what to declutter yourself with. Some things can be sold, some given away to friends or relatives, some donated to a charity and some thrown in the trash. Be careful to shred papers with personal and confidential information.

- ☐ Playbills
- ☐ Reader's Digests
- ☐ National Geographics
- ☐ Harvard Business Reviews
- ☐ Old magazines of "historic" nature
- ☐ Old newspapers of "historic" events
- ☐ Your magazine pile you haven't been able to get to
- ☐ Stamp, coin, baseball card or similar collection
- ☐ Art
- ☐ Books
- ☐ High School and College notebooks
- ☐ Old diaries
- ☐ Trophies from your childhood
- ☐ Halloween costumes
- ☐ Clothing, shoes and hats you haven't worn in 42 years
- ☐ Boxes with stuff you haven't looked at in 12 years
- ☐ Old tax records, receipts, cancelled checks and brokerage statements (see chapter on what records you should retain)
- ☐ Old insurance policies
- ☐ Plastic gifts baskets, ribbons and wrapping papers
- ☐ Dolls and teddy bears that lost their sentimentality
- ☐ Old pet carriers (you haven't had a dog or cat for 9 years!)

- ☐ Expired prescription and over the counter drugs and toiletries and your toothbrush collection from your infrequent dentist visits over the last 50 years
- ☐ Partially filled liquor bottles you haven't touched in years
- ☐ Old cameras
- ☐ Things and stuff
- ☐ _____
- ☐ _____
- ☐ _____
- ☐ _____

If in doubt—Declutter!

WORKSHEET 14

PASSWORDS

Name of person that has information that is not listed here_____

URL or item	User Name	Password	Special comments
Computer			
Cell phone			
External disk backup			

UPDATES TO THIS BOOK

Updates, forms and new worksheets will be posted at www.edwardmendlowitz.com.

Readers with questions or comments can email the author at emendlowitz@withum.com